*f*P

THE FREE PRESS

New York   London   Toronto   Sydney   Singapore

CAPITALIZE ON
MERGER
CHAOS

Six Ways to Profit from
Your Competitors' Consolidation
——And Your Own——

THOMAS M. GRUBB
ROBERT B. LAMB

THE FREE PRESS
A Division of Simon & Schuster, Inc.
1230 Avenue of the Americas
New York, NY 10020

Designed by Carla Bolte

Manufactured in the United States of America

10   9   8   7   6   5   4   3   2   1

Library of Congress Cataloging-in-Publication Data Is Available

Grubb, Thomas M.
    Capitalize on merger chaos : six ways to profit from your competitors'
consolidation and your own / Thomas M. Grubb, Robert B. Lamb.
        p.   cm.
    Includes index.
    1. Consolidation and merger of corporations. 2. Competition.
    3. Strategic alliances (Business) I. Lamb, Robert, 1941- II. Title.
    HD2746.5 .G78 2000
658.1'6—dc21   00-026497

ISBN 0–684–86777–X

With love to Betty, for unending patience and understanding, and to my parents, for everything. —Tom Grubb

This book is dedicated with love to my wife, Nancy Lamb, my son, Roland Lamb, and my daughter, Helena Lamb. —Robert Lamb

Acknowledgments

The authors wish to thank the many corporate executives, managers, and specialists who shared their professional experiences and insights with us. We are very grateful to them as well as to a number of business school professors, management consultants, and key experts in a variety of fields who have been generous in their time, advice, and help over the years this book was being developed and written. We cannot thank everyone individually, but we do wish to acknowledge our gratitude to the following people: William Guth, Dale Zand, Ari Ginsberg, Richard Freedman, William Starbuck, David Rogers, Hrash Bedrosian, Raghu Garud, John Czepiel, Joel Steckel, Myles Shaver, Francis Milliken, Teresa Lant, Steven Mezias, Roy Smith, Ingo Walter, Zur Shapiro, Thomas Pugel, Thomas Gladwin, Charles Fombrun, Roger Dunbar, Paul Shirvastiva, Zenas Bloch, Michael Moses, Bruce Buchanan, Martin Gruber, Edwin Elton, William Silber, Aswath Damodaran, Lawrence White, Paul Wachtel, Praveen Nayyar, Marti Subragmanyam, Michael Uretsky, Ajit Kambil, Lawrence Zicklin, Frederick Gluck, Henry Mintzberg, Peter Lorange, James Brian Quinn, Alfred Rappaport, Michael Porter, C. K. Prahalad, David Nadler, Jeffrey Greene, Thomas Dunfee, David Becker, Steven Usher, David Darst, David Denoon, Richard Pious, Paul Lachman, Melvin Simensky, Lanning Breyer, Gregory Marks, Thomas Dickerson,

Acknowledgments

Thomas Herman, Humphrey Taylor, Robert Teitleman, John Dutton, George Daly, Richard West, Ronald Berenbeim, William May, William Dill, Mark Sirower, Bruce Henderson, Oscar Ornati, Pam Williams, Mark Decker, Rich Escherich, Jeannine La Barbera, Phillip Johnson, Peter Murphy, David Warshaw, Al Vogl, Matthew Budman, Tim Allaway, Deirdre Clark, Sharon Shelley, Ken Kasman, Robert Reich, and Lester Thurow. Finally, many thanks to our partners at The Free Press, including Anne-Marie Sheedy, Linnea Johnson, Carol de Onís, our editor Bob Wallace, and publisher Paula Duffy.

Contents

Introduction

"I gotta believe these guys handed us a huge gift."

—Michael Dell, on Compaq's acquisition of Digital Equipment Corporation

Dell Computer Corporation is firing on all cylinders. Through a series of simultaneous strategic sales, marketing, and operational attacks, coupled with strategic alliances and a thoughtfully deliberated acquisition, Michael Dell is crushing his fiercest competition. Dell knows the rapidly consolidating computer industry is not only teeming with land mines for the unwary, but is also swimming in a wealth of strategic opportunities like no other time in its history. Dell is capitalizing on merger chaos to create record-breaking revenue and profits.

THE RACE FOR NUMBER ONE

Leaping ahead of direct market competitors by stealing their market share and profitability has long been the most deeply imbedded motivation of most firms. However, hitting that highest goal is rare. The vast majority of firms flounder as also-rans, locked into the competitive pack with many others. The business media continually spotlight supposed market leaders—yet, only for the most unique, insightful, talented, and driven companies (like Dell) will the crown of "industry leader" become truly a reality. There can be only one market leader at any one point in time—so how can you turn the tables and become that front-runner if your firm is locked into the crowded pack of followers? *Ironically, today's continuous record-breaking levels of mergers and acquisitions present your firm with an astonishing new wealth of opportunities to break away from competitors like no other time in business history.* For your firm to win in the consolidating world, you must not miss the chance to exploit this abundance of opportunities.

This book gives your team six key strategies that provide a powerful framework for your company to race past competitors during tidal waves of global acquisitions. By executing the right combination of strategies both to capitalize on the merger chaos of competitors and to thrust your own firm forward, your firm can outpace its industry to win in today's fast consolidating world.

Like a rocket freeing itself from the earth's gravitational pull, becoming number one in today's global business is certainly difficult, complex, and fast-changing. Yet, your strategies must also diminish the gravitational pull created by the competition that keeps your firm locked into the pack. Only through the *simultaneous* combination of your firm's strategic thrust and operational speed, and the successful weakening of your competitors' grasp can you vault into the lead and then sustain your escape velocity. When you exploit competitors, you gain extra fuel to propel your escape. If you don't, you may well become fuel for *their* escape.

In 1998, Dell took full advantage of merger chaos and distractions at its direct competitor Compaq Computer Corp., which was struggling to digest Digital Equipment Corp. Michael Dell expressed his delight about the Compaq/Digital merger: "I gotta believe these guys handed us a huge gift."[1] Dell understood the absolute necessity of looking at his industry with a broad sweeping view in order to understand and take full advantage of this new strategic offering Compaq had placed at his doorstep. The typical merger or acquisition creates years of distractions and derails the strategic and operational focus of the combining companies. Dell knew the Compaq/Digital marriage would be no exception. He had to strike quickly to exploit

Dell's Big Climb Past Compaq

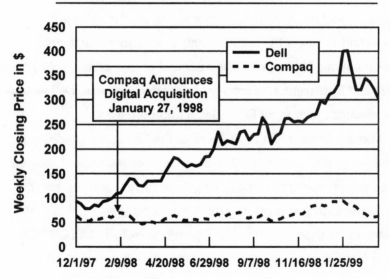

Source: Yahoo!Finance

Note: Weekly closing prices reflect the total accumulated value of one share held on 12/1/97

3

Compaq's merger distraction. Dell launched a barrage of marketing and sales attacks that took dead aim at Compaq's market-leading position, especially in the lucrative business PC market.

In order to capture giant corporate customers from IBM, Compaq believed it must fully integrate all of Digital, a once-great company that had lost market share to more nimble competitors and struggled to barely break even in 1997. This was a grave mistake. Just as countless other acquiring firms have learned, the integration proved to be far more difficult and distracting than Compaq had anticipated. Within just five months Dell had pulled into a dead heat with Compaq as the number one U.S. PC maker. Compaq's 1998 second quarter domestic growth rate was 11 percent while Dell registered a stunning 72 percent jump. By the end of 1998 the effect of Dell's non-merger strategy in the hypercompetitive PC market was clear. Dell's strategic prowess helped it sprint ahead of Compaq and all other competitors as the vendor of choice in the important business PC market. Their 1998 stock value increased a jaw-dropping 248.5 percent, as sales and profits increased 53 percent and 56 percent, respectively.[2] In just over one year, Dell would be crowned the outright PC leader in the entire world.

Michael Dell's initial assessment of the Compaq/Digital merger as a "huge gift" was perfectly described. Compaq's board showed their disappointment at the mismanaged merger and the resulting 71 percent drop in operating profits in 1998, and rightfully held Compaq managers accountable. Top executives, including CEO Eckhard Pfeiffer, each saw their 1998 stock option bonuses cut by at least 50 percent.[3] Soon after, Pfeiffer was terminated, with no new CEO appointed.

However, Michael Dell knew that no single strategy would allow his own company to sustain its dominance over the crowded PC manufacturers' market. In a stunning press release, Dell announced it would buy $16 billion of PC components from rival IBM in the years from 1999 to 2005. The logic of such a deal with a direct competitor may seem baffling at first. But consider each firm's industry-leading strengths. IBM has a computer technology R&D machine that is second to none and has the largest portfolio of patents of any company in the computer industry. Dell owns the industry standard business model for supply chain efficiency. Dell wins because they gained access to IBM's vast R&D machine. IBM wins because they become the key parts provider to the fastest growing computer company in the world.

Michael Dell and IBM CEO Louis Gerstner forged this cooperation strategy because they saw it as a way to quickly leverage and fully utilize both firms' strengths. Gerstner, like Dell, also saw that PCs were becoming more and more commodity-like with quickly shrinking profit margins and forecasts for only single digit growth. Many other firms would have looked at a merger or acquisition as the only avenue for direct competitors to work together. But Dell and Gerstner both knew that quickly teaming up without using a merger to leverage their two organizations' unique resources and greatest strengths would give both firms better long-term financial returns. By October 1999, they signed yet another seven-year deal for IBM to provide Dell with high-end corporate computer services and networks that use Unix, not Microsoft's Windows NT. "This is the nail in the coffin for somebody like Compaq," said U.S. Bancorp Piper Jaffray analyst Ashok Kumar. "It completely neutralizes Compaq's DEC acquisition."[4]

There were 2,900 technology-related U.S. mergers in the first six months of 1999 alone, nearly double the 1998 rate. Michael Dell knows his opportunities were there for easy taking. The attacks on Compaq and the deals with IBM, in fact, were just the start. Because Dell's supply chain management and PC assembly expertise far exceed that of its industry competitors, Michael Dell would be short-sighted if he did not position his company to expand its range of offerings far beyond the PC. As a final assembler of electronic sub-assemblies, no firm is better than Dell. It is not hard to imagine a much longer-term alliance with IBM—one where Dell becomes the assembly, distribution, and marketing ally of the industry's flagship R&D firm.

Additionally, just two days before the first IBM announcement, Dell opened its Gigabyte.com Internet retail store and began selling over thirty thousand different electronic products through its Web site. But Michael Dell wasn't finished in his quest to create long-term sustained market advantages. Dell joined forces with other top technology firms Microsoft Corp., Lycos Inc., and Excite At Home Corp. to pool their vast resources and market reach to directly attack the Internet auction market lead by eBay Inc. Along with the on-line auction experts at start-up Fairmarket, Inc., this top-shelf alliance was the first serious threat to eBay's huge market dominance in the Internet auction industry.

And finally, in September 1999 Dell announced its very first acquisition, buying ConvergeNet Technologies, Inc. The acquisition gave Dell a critical server-based data storage technology that works with a variety of operating systems, from Microsoft Windows to Unix to Linux. Dell's servers could then work with any other server made by competing manufacturers. This key technology developed by ConvergeNet was critical to the flexibility and user friendliness of Dell's servers. The acquisition was not done without vast amounts of research and careful planning. The ConvergeNet addition perfectly filled a technology gap in Dell's exploding server business.

Dell now stands firmly at a critical high-tech intersection. It is poised to grow through its assembly skill, its distribution skill, and its broad marketing skill. One fact is becoming clear, however—*Dell is no longer just about PCs.* Only time will tell what will ultimately unfold from the creative mind—and the creative team—of Michael Dell as he leads his company with a sweeping collection of strategies. Dell's skilled execution of its own consolidation strategies coupled with the simultaneous exploitation of Dell's combining competitors will fuel its continued escape from the crowd.

THE NEW PANORAMIC PERSPECTIVE

For decades, most business strategy has focused on static models—snapshots of firms or industries at one moment in time. This book is entirely different because it uses today's massive worldwide convergence of industries and markets as a continually changing competitive arena with a never-ending bounty of strategic opportunities. In order for you to best utilize and fully exploit the strategies and tools we present in here, *you must first understand and embrace a new panoramic view of business dynamics in today's rapidly converging industries.* Like Michael Dell, you can achieve true market leadership—not only by exploiting the vulnerabilities of merging competitors, but also by identifying, enhancing, and sustaining each of your key competitive advantages, while continually leveraging your firm's growth off the resources of others.

Imagine viewing the entire world and its competitive business landscape simultaneously through the strongest telescope and the most powerful microscope. With this capability, you can broadly see the competitive, strategic, operational, and information links between firms throughout the world. You can see how industries overlap and converge. You can recognize the new business application opportunities created by the invention of new technologies and reapplications of existing ones. You see companies in the process of reinventing themselves to meet changing economic and competitive threats.

But it is also vital for you to see in minute detail the dynamic interworkings of the most successful businesses throughout the world, as well as the greatest causes of failures. You must see simultaneously the key strengths and many weaknesses in both your firm and your competitors. The panoramic perspective allows you to understand the myriad of distractions companies encounter during merger or acquisition integration. You can witness the fear and anxiety of employees at the announcement that their company has been sold to a competitor. You learn the causes of clashing cultures and the daily battle between business practices as two companies struggle to find some order during their merger of "equals."

This book's view of many industries' forced convergence is sweeping and comprehensive, but exacting and detailed at the same time. Because today's global business landscape changes constantly, it is critical that you put the world under constant surveillance using this panoramic outlook. *Only* then can you outpace competitors during the rampant consolidation taking place in countless industries.

In short, only your team's constant vigilance over competitors' threats and vulnerabilities can enable your firm to achieve and sustain its continued competitive advantages.

MERGER MANIA, MERGER FAILURE

In 1999, world-wide merger volume jumped 36 percent to $3.4 trillion, racing forward at a stunning $1.6 billion per business hour. U.S. merger volume rose to a record $1.75 trillion while Europe exploded more than doubling to $1.23 trillion, capped by Vodaphone Airtouch's $181 billion hostile takeover of Mannesmann, the largest in history.[5] Since 1992, every year has rewritten the record for merger volume. U.S. volume totaled $6.5 trillion in the 1990s. More than half this volume occurred in 1998 and 1999 alone. Only time will tell when the current global consolidation run will lose steam, but it will not happen anytime soon.

By January 2000, it was clear to see the M&A steamroller was still pushing forward. America Online announced the biggest acquisition in U.S. history—initially valued at $183 billion—of media and cable giant Time Warner.[6] Just a few days later, Europe's Glaxo Wellcome and SmithKline Beecham announced their $76 billion merger, creating the world's largest drug company. Soon after, Pfizer won a takeover battle against American Home Products, winning the right to acquire Warner-Lambert for $93.4 billion, creating a pharmaceutical giant valued at over $230 billion. (See Appendices A and B for a summary of U.S. and global transactions by size and trend.)

In fact, although companies in all industries are joining together at ever increasing record rates, *the sobering reality is that only about 20 per-*

Global M&A Activity

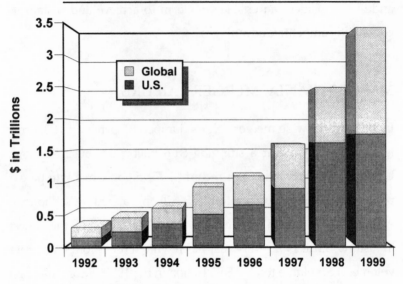

Source: Securities Data Company

cent of all mergers and acquisitions really succeed. Most mergers typically erode shareholder wealth, create years of chaos, fear, and turmoil for their employees, and take a medley of missteps to perfectly position themselves to lose the battle against their direct market competitors.

While mergers are the largest capital expenditures most companies ever make, they are frequently the worst planned and executed business activities of all. According to McKinsey & Co., nearly 80 percent of all mergers fail to recover the costs incurred in the deal. Fully half result in reduced productivity, profits, or both.[7] Warren Hellman, former head of Lehman Brothers, stated, "So many mergers fail to deliver what they promise that there should be a presumption of failure. The burden of proof should be on showing that anything really good is likely to come out of one."[8] The latest tidal wave of merger activity is doing exactly what past tidal waves have done—hide the cold, hard reality *that most mergers fail to achieve any real financial returns.* However, for your company, armed with our six strategies to profit from both competitors' and your own consolidations, this huge global merger failure rate becomes a very exciting discovery.

A Long History of Merger Failure

Merger failure is not a recent phenomenon nor is it a single isolated measurement at one moment in time. A continuing pattern of merger and acquisition failures has been well-documented since 1950.[9] (See Appendix C for a comprehensive list of merger and acquisition studies conducted from 1950 to 1999.) Warren Hellman made a courageous statement. He has absolutely nothing to gain by departing from the investment banking community and laying out the cards face up on the table for all to see. When you contemplate joining the M&A game you should heed his words—they provide an absolute truth from an expert who is positioned to know the truth.

But like the teenager who is oblivious to the proven accident rates of teenage drivers, most firms jump naively into the merger fray with little or no understanding of what troubles lie hidden in their future. (See Appendix D to learn about the array of forces driving consolidation.) Traditional wisdom states, "Eat or be eaten, or hide your head in the sand and hope for the best." This reflects a *totally* inadequate view of the vast array of strategic opportunities offered up during waves of massive consolidation. Traditional wisdom's assessment of the very high positive value of mergers and acquisitions is also extremely dangerous for the firm that embraces it, because it usually results in deep disappointments and may well drag that company down into financial ruin.

Warren Buffett stated that firms adopt the irresistible urge to buy a company because everyone else is doing it.[10] This herd mentality can lead the most successful and well-intentioned firms down a path to corporate destruction.

Merger mania is dangerous for at least three reasons. First, it hides true merger failure rates and promotes squandering of valuable corporate and human resources. Second, it causes tunnel vision that diverts most managers from the real strategic opportunities their firms have to beat the competition. Your firm's nonmerger strategies and other alternatives are often far better ways to gain advantages over your rivals that blindly jump into the M&A game.

Third, *no* firm is exempt from the impact of the changing competitive landscape resulting from massive consolidation. Even if your industry is not consolidating, the impact of mergers, acquisitions, joint ventures, and strategic alliances in other industries—which may be closely related or seem only vaguely related to yours—may create a devastating, entirely new competitive threat to your business.

The very high rate of merger failure creates the foundation for our six strategies and our panoramic view. Your team must understand the chaos, turmoil, distractions, and financial failure created in the typical merger situation—they provide the critical imperative that your team must do very careful preplanning and precision execution in your own acquisitions, mergers, or merger alternatives, *if they are to have a chance of success.* Only when you clearly understand the devastating impact of merger failure can you see the *gold mine* of strategic opportunities available to capitalize on the chaos of your merging competitors.

1

Six Ways to Profit
from Consolidation

The most beautiful diamonds are cut in an intricate pattern of multiple facets. Under a spotlight, each facet plays upon every other to create the most radiance. The gem cutter's expertise shines through when the design is perfectly planned and the facets skillfully cut to elicit the utmost light and brilliance from the stone. Strong business leaders in the consolidating world are much like the expert diamond cutter. Managers must understand the multifaceted nature of their competitive arena and craft strategic and operational plans to create the best chance of success for the business and wealth for shareholders. They must be able to see facets their competitors ignore. They must be armed with an array of tools and use them in the proper combination to capture the vast opportunities served up by the consolidating world.

A CRUCIAL CAUSE OF MERGER FAILURE

According to a Boston Consulting Group study, many firms fail to do adequate pre-merger integration planning.[1] They found that eight of ten acquiring companies do *no* pre-merger planning or analysis of the target company's business practices, staff, skills, structure or organization design, sources of core competencies, and its range of tangible and intangible resources for growth. Most mergers underperform because top managers fail to consider the specific steps required to integrate an acquisition into their company or analyze how they will maximize their joint potential. You don't need to dig too deep to uncover an eerie correlation between the 80 percent of firms who do no pre-merger planning and the almost 80 percent of mergers that fail to meet their minimal financial goals.

Rampant merger failure presents your firm with a new wealth of strategic opportunities. Our strategies are your key to achieve and maintain your escape from the swarm of direct market competitors. These six strategies will enable your firm to profit from *all* consolidation—both yours *and* your competitors'.

STRATEGY 1: THE MAGNET STRATEGY

Poorly planned and badly executed merger integration creates fear, anger, and uncertainty among employees and managers. Employees of the acquired firm often feel they've been sold out. They need someone to want them and to reestablish a trusting bond. This someone can be a strong competitor firm like yours which is not involved in merger mania.

Your firm can use the magnet strategy to attract a merging competitor's top talent who are often so anxious to flee their company's merger chaos, they may actively seek out your team. This strategy generates key additional human and intellectual resources that give you the ability to stride ahead while simultaneously hollowing out the talent pool of competitor firms, pushing them further back into the pack.

For example, in late 1998, just after Deutsche Bank's chairman Rolf Breuer boldly announced, "There will be no autonomy" for its Banker's Trust/Alex Brown acquisition, many acquired employees used this suffocating statement as their rallying cry to escape the merger chaos. They ran into the arms of welcoming competitors, including Credit Suisse First Boston, Tucker Anthony Inc., and T. Rowe Price. Six out of eleven of BT Alex Brown's highest ranking executives, along with entire branch offices and practice groups, were easily recruited away by direct competitors.

The magnet strategy creates a double win—your competitor is weakened at the same time your firm gains strength. Drawing highly capable people directly from your *merging* competitors is a much more powerful win. In fact, even a start-up company can be staffed directly from the talent pools of competitor firms mired in merger chaos.

In Chapter 2, we show how huge firms like Procter & Gamble, General Electric, and Citigroup, along with small firms like Houston Community Bank and Sassaby, Inc., can either use or fall victim to the magnet strategy. Houston Community Bank increased its business by 33 percent in just one year using the magnet strategy—all at the expense of larger banks in the midst of merger chaos.

STRATEGY 2: ATTACK WHILE COMPETITORS ARE DISTRACTED

Another vital non-merger strategy firms can use to beat their merging competitors is to time strategic attacks against them precisely when those firms are most vulnerable—when they are floundering in the chaos of merger or acquisition integration. Most merging companies lose their ability even to see—much less to respond to—another firm's sudden strategic attack against their business. Such well-timed attacks on stalled mergers can steal market share, customers, suppliers, distributors, and alliance partners, transferring critical velocity directly to your company. While Boeing was struggling in near total chaos with its McDonnell Douglas acquisition, Europe's Airbus Industrie quickly attacked Boeing's huge market share. Within twenty-four months Airbus completely reversed the market dominance in this worldwide duopoly. When Boeing bought McDonnell Douglas, it owned 65 percent of the entire commercial aircraft market. In the first six months of 1999, the attacks on Boeing's leadership position allowed *Airbus* to capture 66 percent of all orders in the world.

The difficult work of merger integration can be all-consuming, and the normal tendency in combining firms is to lose at least part of their external vision because they are forced to focus inward on immediate acquisition or integration problems. Just as in war, your corporate attacks are most effective when the enemy isn't looking, is distracted, or can't respond. As demonstrated in the Introduction, a great portion of Dell Computer's recent overwhelming success has come directly at the expense of Compaq, as that firm struggles to digest Digital Equipment Corp.

In Chapter 3, we look at how many firms, including Airbus, Pepsi-Co, Wal-Mart, and Burlington Northern Santa Fe, have used precisely timed strategic attacks to gain critical velocity needed to outrun competitors paralyzed in merger turmoil.

STRATEGY 3: JUMP START VITAL INTERNAL CHANGE

Your team must use the threatened mergers by your direct competitors to jump-start major change inside your firm. Often, there is no more powerful force to drive your entire company's vital update and transformation than a direct competitor's merger announcement. This strategy is specifically designed to power your firm's forward momentum by maximizing your own team's current internal resources, talents, and motivation. For example, AT&T's new CEO Michael Armstrong used the powerful direct threat created by the mega-merger of MCI and WorldCom as a catalyst to energize AT&T into action like no other time in the company's history. The entire organization attacked out-of-control costs, eliminating $5 billion per year of unnecessary expense. This allowed AT&T to free up huge cash flow for many major global initiatives, including joint ventures, acquisitions, and technology upgrades.

Chapter 4 shows how the remarkable transformation at corporate giants Ford, AT&T, Honda, and Toyota was triggered by the threat created by combining competitors. These companies propelled themselves into market-leading positions in market share, profit, or shareholder wealth by jump starting critical internal changes.

STRATEGY 4: MERGER ALTERNATIVES

Your firm's joint ventures, strategic alliances, franchising, and licensing agreements often multiply your potential universe of resources by leveraging those of all your partners. These key co-ventures quickly help your firm to accelerate its forward momentum because many different agreements can be entered into simultaneously. The benefits from such partnerships are often derived much faster, cheaper, easier, more profitably, and without the debilitating conflict and turmoil when compared to a typical merger or acquisition. Microsoft's huge dominance over Apple Computer was a direct result of Microsoft's ability—and Apple's *inability or unwillingness*—to forge a massive network of joint ventures and licensing agreements.

In most mergers the acquiring firm buys the equivalent of a six-foot-long sandwich which contains certain desired items, but also numerous *undesired* items which either must be sold off, carried at a loss, or thrown away. These undesired parts of the acquired company may confuse the buying organization and distract top management attention. More important, these non-core, largely extraneous parts often force the acquirer to bid an excessively expensive price for the acquisition, not because they ever wanted to buy those pieces, but because those pieces are deemed to have a current market value to other potential bidders. In contrast, most strategic alliances, joint ventures, or licensing deals are focused only on the *needed pieces* of the business. They normally do not require expensive investment bankers, are negotiated directly by the two companies, and do not involve extraneous items or non-core businesses, nor the payment of exorbitant acquisition control price premiums. Firms can "cherry pick" desired items and specifically exclude others in order to build a mutual competitive advantage.

In Chapter 5, we explore the merger alternative strategies that have propelled many firms into market leadership, including Microsoft, Motorola, NEC, and the members of the giant global airline Star Alliance.

STRATEGY 5: FAST-TRACK MERGER INTEGRATION

No manager has ever overestimated the difficulty of integrating two companies. Merger integration is so very difficult because you only get one chance to do it right. *There are no test runs.* By streamlining and accelerating the process, you minimize the loss of key managers and skilled technicians, the erosion of morale, and the likelihood of merger chaos. When your firm executes a fast-track, well-planned merger integration, you multiply its chance of success when compared to the typical merging firm. Your team's critical forward momentum will be accelerated through a planned fast-track integration, allowing a faster escape from the grasp of market competitors. General Electric's market leadership in all areas of its business and stratospheric $500 billion market value have been a direct result of successful integration of over six hundred acquisitions during the watch of CEO Jack Welch. Through its comprehensive strategy of lightning-quick acquisitions, Cisco Systems surpassed Microsoft to become the world's most valuable company in March of 2000. Both Cisco and GE created fast-track integration processes which they both continually improve as a corporate core competency that allows them to stay ahead of their competitors. Many firms are now copying their merger models.

Fast-track integration directly attacks two key reasons for merger failure. First, they are often entered into with no clear plan for how to best integrate the people, systems, and operations of the two firms. Second, most merger integrations take far too long. And the longer they take, the more nonproductive energy the combined organization uses up, the higher most workers' uncertainty, the greater the distraction of top leaders' attention from productive work, and the greater the probability of failure. Merger failure guarantees a huge additional gravitational force bearing down upon your firm, preventing forward momentum and profitability.

Expertly executed merger integration clearly defines the exact business units, systems, and practices that will be melded into one. Of equal importance, the business components that will remain *autonomous* are also clearly planned and communicated to the new organization. Chapter 6 introduces a full array of foundations and integration tools you must use to create—in advance of the merger announcement—a crystal-clear plan integrating the two firms quickly and successfully. We look at examples of companies, including General Electric, Southwest Airlines, and Swiss Bank Corp., that executed their merger and acquisition integration and actually accelerated their forward momentum, achieving the necessary speed to outrun the competition.

STRATEGY 6: COMPOSITE STRATEGY

The best global growth firms simply cannot sprint past their competitors using a single strategy. The world is far too complex and fast-changing for any old-fashioned static strategy to work. Thus, your firm's selection of the best composite strategy is the ultimate weapon to captilize on merger chaos. To most effectively profit from all aspects of rampant consolidation, you must link together the key set of dynamic strategies available to your firm. Your team can exploit others' merger chaos and keep those firms pushed into the pack of market competitors while simultaneously driving forward your own winning mergers, acquisitions, or merger alternatives. By executing two or more clear strategies that others tend to ignore or execute poorly, you gain speed to race faster than the competition.

In today's technologically fast-changing business environment, the windows of opportunity for strategic attacks often are open only briefly and close quickly. More importantly, if you do not exploit an opportunity, your direct competitors *will*. This turns the tables, giving them additional resources, time, market share, and profits. There are no neutral choices here.

Complex competitive multinational environments, in particular, always require a composite strategy to vault beyond the pack. In just eighteen months, Michael Armstrong completely transformed AT&T from a slow-moving long-distance telephone bureaucracy into a potential Internet juggernaut, using a complicated series of acquisitions, global alliances, strategic attacks, internal changes, and several key merger alternatives.

Today's rapidly converging industries drive the momentum of change and, for most firms, create an imperative for flexibility and require a multiple strategy approach. By learning how to use and to combine the options available in our first five key strategies—(1) creating a magnet strategy to exploit merging competitors, (2) attacking while competitors are distracted by merger chaos, (3) jump-starting internal change, (4) using multiple merger alternatives, and (5) fast-track acquisitions or mergers—you develop essential skills

21

for dynamic flexibility. However, you and your team must create a unique composite strategy by combining two or more of these strategies to best exploit the vast array of current opportunities offered in your industry. You can only win in the consolidating world if you accurately identify, assess, and implement the most appropriate specific strategy for each market. You must develop the versatility to combine different groupings of our strategies, coupled with others unique to your situation, *simultaneously when necessary.*

Chapter 7 demonstrates how market leaders, including The Home Depot, Toyota, Procter & Gamble, AT&T, British Airways, and General Electric, all depend upon complex composite strategies. They exploit every opportunity to both capitalize on merging competitors and drive forward with their own consolidations.

THE DOUBLE-EDGED SWORD

These six strategies are your key for exploiting the vast new opportunities created by record levels of mergers and acquisitions. But you must embrace a panoramic perspective of the world around you. An "eat or be eaten" outlook guarantees you will miss out on many prime strategic opportunities created by many consolidating industries. These strategies are your key for racing past and staying ahead of the competition—your key to profit from tidal waves of consolidation.

In the combining industry, you must succeed *and* you must not fail. The rewards of successful mergers, merger alternatives, and non-merger strategies can be so enormous and the damage of losing so destructive that you must be ever-vigilant to do both—*win and not lose.* Much like the hand-to-hand, to-the-death gladiator

The Double-Edged Sword

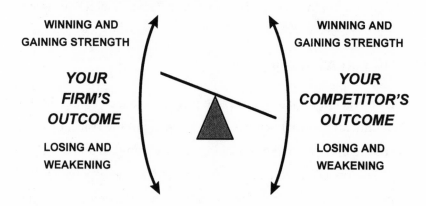

WINNING AND
GAINING STRENGTH

*YOUR
FIRM'S
OUTCOME*

LOSING AND
WEAKENING

WINNING AND
GAINING STRENGTH

*YOUR
COMPETITOR'S
OUTCOME*

LOSING AND
WEAKENING

battles of times past, often there is only one outcome that will allow your firm to become a market leader.

When your firm wins on the consolidation battlefield you are rewarded with a major source of competitive advantage. But severe injury results from failed mergers and you place massive self-imposed gravitational forces on your firm. The merger process confronts any company with a risk-versus-reward tradeoff that is like a dynamic fulcrum—with *diametrically opposed* outcomes.

If your firm effectively navigates the tidal waves of consolidation, *your benefits are doubled*—you are strengthened financially, organizationally, and reputationally while your competitors are simultaneously weakened. You are handed a double-edged sword, the greatest new strategic weapon in your arsenal.

But this double-edged sword can work *against* you just as it can work for you. When you fail in your strategic and operational navigation you hand the sword to your competitors, who then benefit directly at *your* expense. They steal your momentum, initiatives, and your best employees and block your opportunities. Your mistakes fuel their forward thrust while your firm suffers as a market follower.

THE GREAT ACQUIRER

Your merger or acquisition must be properly planned and executed. Not only do financial benefits come sooner, but the risks of a confused organization and financial losses are minimized and the flight of your top talent can be prevented. Yet the more powerful, far longer-term benefits your firm derives from successful acquisitions stretch well beyond simple rates of return or market share gains. You can virtually create a new vital core competency as a "Great Acquirer" with financial, managerial, and reputational benefits that cascade into the future.

What are the far-reaching advantages to General Electric, Cisco, and Ford, all possessing well-known track records of merger and acquisition excellence? The Great Acquirer gains a "halo effect" which can leverage the firm's limited resources several times over. The well-known skillful acquirer can become the "merger partner of choice." In quickly consolidating industries, like financial services, Great Acquirers are often approached by potential targets. CEOs of target firms openly request to be purchased. Whether these CEOs' motivation is protection from a hostile suitor, or maximization of their own or their shareholders' wealth, they are willing, indeed eager, to jump into the arms of a star quality acquirer.

In early 1999, Ford Motor Company reaped big dividends for being a Great Acquirer. As the consolidating world automotive industry rushed to find suitable partners in the late 1990s, Ford was richly rewarded with the prized and profitable automotive operations of AB Volvo. No explanation of our Great Acquirer concept could be more precisely stated than the Ford/Volvo merger account in *The Wall Street Journal:* "As the smaller auto makers look for bigger partners in the global consolidation of the auto industry, Ford has emerged as the 'acquirer of choice,' industry experts say. That is because the No. 2 auto maker world-wide has a track record of treating its acquisitions well by injecting capital and expertise without diluting a brand's character. The most visible examples are Britain's Jaguar Cars Ltd., which Ford acquired in 1989, and Japan's Mazda Motor Corp., in which Ford holds a controlling one-third stake."[2]

The halo effect develops a self-fulfilling momentum. Great Acquirers are not only approached as white knights in hostile takeover situations, but they are approached with many more attractive opportunities than average firms. Because of the halo, over the long haul, successful acquirers retain far more top managers and the highest skilled employees. Their deep talent pool gives them the needed capability to continually beat their competition.

Additionally, the world is very forgiving in the case of the Great Acquirer. As celebrated as GE is in conducting successful mergers, they have had some terrible disasters. Their acquisitions of Kidder Peabody and Montgomery Ward were miserable failures. Kidder Peabody's trading scheme scandal resulted in a $1.2 billion loss before GE pulled the plug and sold Kidder to PaineWebber.[3] The Montgomery Ward acquisition fared even worse, ending in bankruptcy. But, because GE has such a powerful track record with hundreds of successful acquisitions, investors and Wall Street viewed the Kidder and Montgomery Ward failures as simple aberrations. GE has a positive halo. Faith in GE was never eroded. In fact, GE sits as king of the corporate mountain as *Fortune* magazine's "World's Most Admired Company."

A company possessing a halo of success can turn what otherwise can be a tense hostile merger negotiation and painful integration into a positive, constructive partnership for both firms. This halo effect often speeds the merger process by reducing antagonism and building employee confidence and commitment, and therefore achieves profits far earlier than in the typical corporate acquisition.

The successful acquirer's halo provides its managers with a valuable pre-acquisition negotiation tool—they can use their halo to drive down control price premiums. When target company managers and shareholders see a record of strong merger success and well-executed merger integrations by the acquirer, they are far less likely to demand excessive premiums to accept a deal. Additionally, in the case of stock swaps, target shareholders will be far more inclined to hold onto shares of their new stock than to dump them quickly in the market. Most investors know that the history of merger success and financial gains from this firm with a halo will bring excellent shareholder returns. Because investors are far less inclined to cash out and run, the halo company's stock price remains far more stable during periods of continuing mergers and acquisitions, when compared to less-well-thought-of firms whose stock price tends to fluctuate downward during each merger attempt.

Shareholders of GE's acquisition targets have experienced just this financial success. GE's market capitalization soared to over $500 billion by the end of 1999, making it one of the world's most valuable companies. Part of this drive to GE's record corporation valuation was created by thousands of its acquired company shareholders holding tightly to their newly secured GE shares. When target share-holders see the chance to trade for shares of a Great Acquirer, they do not need huge control price premiums to make the deal palat-able. It is sweet enough already. However, the real power of GE's halo is its crucial strategic leverage, which acts as a financial multi-plier. For example, GE's financial division GE Capital's total of over three hundred mergers and acquisitions purchased at deep financial discounts or almost no acquisition control price premiums has liter-ally produced many hundreds of millions, and in some cases bil-lions, of dollars in combined investment savings and immediately increased profitability to GE each year.

The Negative Halo

Conversely, when a firm earns a reputation as an unacceptable part-ner, it in fact creates a "negative halo" with damages that cascade into the future. All the benefits to the good acquirer are exactly re-versed. It must pay much higher control premiums to have an acqui-sition offer accepted. A firm with a reputation for merger failures multiplies the fears of harm or damage caused by harshly negative synergies. Many firms' gross merger failures have driven them into a "death spiral." The conglomerate graveyards of the 1970s are littered with terminally failed mergers. Many failed mergers lose their com-petitive and forward momentum. Union Pacific railroad alone had seriously damaged its reputation, which they are still trying to repair. Because their poorly managed merger with Southern Pacific had justifiably received enormous negative media coverage for over two years, Union's ability to effectively conduct business in many other arenas was severely diminished.

A firm that earns the reputation as a bad merger partner finds fewer opportunities, not only in additional mergers and acquisitions, but also for strategic alliances, joint ventures, and preferential treatment from customers and suppliers. A diminished ability to attract and retain top talent and an increased cost of capital are the harsh realities of the negative halo.

––––––––––

The following chapters describe the six strategies to *Capitalize on Merger Chaos* in detail. Each strategy can become a facet of your diamond-like overall strategy. When crafted and executed with skill and precision, the brilliance that can be achieved far exceeds the sum of the individual parts. Your strategy must produce the most radiance— the most profits, market share, and shareholder wealth. Only then can you achieve and sustain the ultimate business success—becoming number one in your industry.

2

Create a Magnet Strategy

FISHING IN TROUBLED WATERS

Poorly planned merger or acquisition integration invariably leads to turmoil and chaos. Because more than 80 percent of acquiring companies build *no* up-front integration roadmap, you can very reasonably anticipate that your merging competitors will experience upheaval, uncertainty, and employee fear and frustration. Target employees especially are prone to a collection of anxieties—they feel betrayed by the target company's management and fear the loss of their jobs through cost-cutting efforts of their new employer. They need someone who needs them, someone to rescue them from the chaos of the typical badly managed integration. Seize this moment! This is a perfect opportunity to attract talented employees away from that competitor firm.

What worsens the fear, anger, and confusion generated in mergers and acquisitions is that many executives in the target companies are protected by "change of control" provisions in their employment contracts. This means they receive substantial financial incentives to abandon the target firm when the acquisition is finalized. As Michael Krause, then Tambrand's senior VP of global operations stated immediately after Tambrand's acquisition by Procter & Gamble, "I just want my money so I can get the hell out." When senior executives leave the target after its acquisition, remaining employees (the overwhelming majority with no acquisition parachute) are thrown deeper into uncertainty and anxiety. The top executives to whom they looked to for information, guidance, reassurance, and leadership have essentially deserted them.

The employees of the *acquiring* firm also have reasons to escape the typical merger situation. Along with wanting to flee the confusion and chaos of a long, painful integration, they may be motivated to leave because the average merger runs a 50 percent chance of suffering reduced productivity and profits. Managers and professionals want to avoid the taint of association with corporate decline or financial disaster, as well as the potential of reduced personal performance or reputation caused by the firm's chaotic environment. Additionally, employees whose personal financial rewards are highly dependent upon organization performance fear that their own financial status will suffer from bad acquisitions. Therefore, when you open your arms, employees of both the target and acquiring companies often will come running.

Procter & Gamble lost two highly valued vice-presidents in just such a manner during their acquisition of Noxell Corporation. P&G

veteran John Saxton had been tapped to lead the acquisition. When results did not meet planned expectations, he was reassigned, and before long he was stolen away as CEO of The Sheridan Group. His replacement, Beth Kaplan, was raided by Rite Aid Corporation. Both were fast-track, high potential leaders for P&G, and each was a needed leadership resource of the merger integration. P&G's Noxell integration proved to be even more difficult due to the disruptions caused by the quick exits of these two key leaders and increased uncertainty and confusion among the remaining employees.

Executive recruiters and headhunters have long known about the opportunities created by merging companies and they prey upon the fear and uncertainty created by these firms. They swoop into target firms within hours after a merger announcement, offering promises of more money, and trumpeting their ability to provide stability and security. By elaborating on the horrors of past mergers by this particular acquirer or others they fan the fires of fear, mistrust, and doubt—so they can steal top performers. It is no wonder headhunters use merger and acquisition opportunities as a primary strategy to build their business. They need people who are motivated to jump ship. Fear and anxiety are perfect motivators.

The normal headhunter's fee is 30 percent of a recruit's first-year salary. But your firm can hire these people stricken by merger chaos *without* a headhunter. Your employment offers will not require expensive signing bonuses nor pay premiums since pay is not the primary motivator here. You know exactly what the headhunter knows—it is fear, anxiety, and chaos that drive people to explore an opportunity with another firm. In fact, one of the most crucial benefits of the magnet strategy is that you do not destabilize your current

31

pay scale because you can often continue to hire the best merger refugees without paying exorbitant headhunter fees or huge signing bonuses. This also reinforces your existing employees' sense of the fairness of your firm's pay system. Existing employees feel cheated, angry, and threatened when new "stars" are "bought" with huge signing bonuses or inflated salaries. Salary inflation madness can spread like a virus throughout your organization if each new salary offer to an outsider stretches the high end of a current pay range. Your very best current managers and experts can become so jealous and angry that they willingly take headhunter phone calls urging them to join your competitor for large signing bonuses and salary increases. The magnet strategy of recruiting the very best merger refugees with no headhunter fees or signing bonuses allows your firm to use that money to reward your teams for working to recruit the top refugees. Your teams are thus continually strengthened with new blood that they helped to recruit, and receive incentives via real bonus payments for surveying the continuing merger failures to find refugees who have special expertise and skills that your team needs. Using this magnet strategy, therefore, builds and enriches your team's range of competencies, range of customers, and geographic range of market knowledge. (You must be very alert that your new recruits do not violate noncompetition agreements by joining your firm. This can be a dangerous trap for the unwary. You must not break the law.)

Your firm need only recruit one good manager or specialist from the merging competitor. This first recruit creates a bridge back to his or her previous firm—a bridge for *others* in that merging firm to use. W. Phillip Johnson Jr., chairman of the board and CEO at Houston

Community Bank (HCB), used this strategy to gain a competitive advantage in the Houston banking market. One of HCB's local competitors, Interstate Bank North, was purchased by Compass Bank of Birmingham, Alabama. As part of the purchase agreement, only Interstate's chairman received an employment contract. Interstate's president did not, and his future with Compass was uncertain.

Johnson used this merger of his rivals to win in Houston's market. When Interstate's president was approached by Johnson with a job that offered stability and security, he jumped at the offer to become president of HCB. Thus with no headhunter Johnson was able to raid a direct competitor's top talent. HCB's business increased over 33 percent within the next year. Where did that business originate? *From former clients at Interstate.* By quickly exploiting a competitor's merger, Houston Community Bank won while Interstate and Compass lost. The double-edged sword worked with surgical precision.

Johnson continued to use the Interstate/Compass merger to his advantage. HCB expanded its operation in 1998, and using the bridge built by the former Interstate officer, Johnson recruited another Interstate manager to run this new expansion. Recruiting risk is virtually eliminated when you have such extremely reliable information about the skill and track record of a potential new hire. Furthermore, talent raiding isn't just for small firms like Houston Community Bank. Size is not a barrier. For example, when John Saxton left P&G during its Noxell merger chaos to become CEO of The Sheridan Group, he hired both his new CFO and president of The Sheridan Press unit directly from P&G. Additionally, soon after telecommunications giants SBC Communications Inc. and Ameritech Corp. announced their $56 billion deal, national Internet service provider Verio Inc. stole away Ameritech's head of cellular and paging services business. This strategy is perfect for firms of any size that choose *not* to do mergers, but still aim to win in the consolidating world.

When you successfully recruit good performers away from your merging competitors, you gain a double competitive advantage: you build your firm's strength and forward velocity while simultaneously further weakening your competitors who are losing key people, the ability to work as a well-tuned team, and ever-important "know-how." But even more important, you heighten the probability of that merging organization losing its forward momentum and coherence as a business. You wield the double-edged sword by depriving your competitor of key results producers at a most critical stage of the merging organization's development. Because your company has hired a key person whose head contains the merging firm's core competency, in time, he or she may provide additional competitive advantages to your firm.

BUILD A LONG-TERM MAGNET STRATEGY

Alert managers in non-merging firms should develop skilled teams to exploit these continually recurring failed merger opportunities. With almost 11,000 different consolidations in the United States in 1999 alone, the business landscape is littered with merger chaos and uncertainty. *Even if merger activity stops tomorrow, the ongoing chaos will last for years to come.* Firms who botch their merger or acquisition integrations often see the baggage, tension, and mistrust last for five, ten, or even more years.

You can build a long-term magnet strategy to strengthen your competencies and skill sets by becoming a safe harbor for the best merger refugees. Exploit this dynamic fulcrum like suddenly shifting your weight on a child's seesaw, as the most talented refugees seek out your firm's safe haven and solid team atmosphere. In the financial industry, Morgan Guaranty, Merrill Lynch, and Goldman Sachs avoided most merger waves and became magnets for top talent. You can create a top-level docking station task force to offer a welcoming home and solid team atmosphere in your firm. Your task force must stress the stability of your firm's strategy, structure, and rewards to attract the top talent.

This magnet strategy weakens your competitors just when they are most vulnerable, for the organizational uncertainties of their unfinished acquisition are made worse by the loss of skilled employees and managers around whom they hoped to build. It usually takes that competitor firm much more time to recruit new people and to get its merger up to the planned level of growth and business success. Your competitor may well now lose other good managers and employees who feel even less inclined to stay at a firm that allows this painful uncertainty to continue and its best managers to flee. A downward spiral of defections set in. The result—*your competitor bleeds talent.*

The purpose of the magnet strategy is not to steal trade secrets, nor is it a thin veil for corporate espionage. Instead, it is specifically designed to create a long-term ongoing process to leverage the continuing chaos of the consolidating world. It provides a continuous source of fuel to propel your firm past all competitors. The push for strategic bigness, fast globalization, and revenue growth virtually guarantees this merger wave's future well into this 21st century and ensures a continuing supply of people looking for a safe harbor.

Your magnet strategy is not static nor rigid, but dynamic. You can—*and must*—periodically readjust its focus to attract new types of required specialties and talents. You can cross industry borders to target highly desirable functional experts. For example, in specific labor shortages such as that in Information Technology, the annual college graduate supply is 75 percent below current needs.[1] The magnet strategy can become a critical source of competitive advantage in many industries by attracting very scarce IT professionals directly from the many firms who are engulfed in merger turmoil. You can tailor the strategy into a key component of your overall recruiting system by refocusing on new skills your firm will target to acquire from among each year's best merger refugees.

Sun Microsystems solved its problem of finding enough qualified IT professionals by transforming its entire work force into the ultimate magnet. Sun paid $1,000 to each person who successfully recruited an IT employee into the company. The result for Sun was a dramatic 25 percent decrease in recruiting costs while it attracted a large group of new star employees in the midst of the ferociously competitive IT job market.

Sandy Weill, co-CEO at Citigroup (created from the merger of Travelers and Citicorp in 1998) is well aware of the force possessed by the magnet strategy. When Jamie Dimon shocked the financial industry with his sudden exit from Citigroup, Weill knew that Dimon, his former right-hand man and for years his heir apparent, could become a powerful magnet to draw many top executives away from Citigroup. As part of Dimon's separation settlement, Weill insisted that he agree not to hire any Citigroup, Salomon Smith Barney, or Travelers Insurance employees for three years. Weill knew that he needed all hands on deck to have a chance of making the difficult Travelers/Citicorp union a success. From the time the Citigroup merger was announced, its stock price fell by more than 50 percent within six months. Financial services firms, especially banks like Citicorp that had large loan losses across all of Asia, Latin America, and Russia, were hurting, and Sandy Weill knew it was in his best interest to try to keep the double-edged sword out of the hands of Jamie Dimon if he and co-CEO John Reed were able to have a chance of turning around Citigroup by holding the best teams in place. Weill's decisive action worked, and by late 1999 Citigroup's stock was trading at record highs.

EXPAND YOUR BUSINESS OR START AN ENTIRELY NEW ONE

When Baltimore-based Alex Brown, the oldest financial brokerage firm in the United States, was bought by Bankers Trust in 1997 (and then by Deutsche Bank in 1998) several direct competitors jumped at the opportunity to expand their operations in the Baltimore market *at Alex Brown's expense.* Tucker Anthony, Inc. opened an office in Annapolis, Maryland, staffed exclusively with former Alex Brown executives and brokers recruited directly from Alex Brown's Annapolis office. As a result, Alex Brown was forced to close the doors on their Annapolis operation. Tucker's magnet strategy not only pulled valuable employees from Alex Brown, but it also landed the sumptuous prize of $1 billion in assets under management.

Credit Suisse First Boston stole away with four managing directors and thirty other Alex Brown employees in order to open a Baltimore-based health care investing unit. A similar operation at Alex Brown had produced annual revenue exceeding $100 million. The dynamic fulcrum of the double-edged sword will fill First Boston's corporate pockets with revenues equal to the revenue loss at Alex Brown. And finally, Donaldson, Lufkin & Jenrette, a New York brokerage, opened an office in Baltimore staffed with just one former Alex. Brown managing director. There is little doubt more Alex Brown employees will soon be working for DLJ in Baltimore.

Sassaby, Inc. also used the magnet strategy as a powerful start-up tool when it launched *Jane,* a new mass marketed brand of cosmetics designed for teenagers. The unit was staffed—from its birth in 1994—with merger refugees. Soon after Noxell Corporation was acquired by Procter & Gamble, Sassaby partnered with key refugee managers to develop an entirely new cosmetic brand to compete head-to-head with the industry's entrenched stalwarts like Cover Girl (the acquired P&G brand), Maybelline, and Revlon.

Sassaby was amazed to learn the extraordinary usefulness of the merger refugee bridge back to P&G. In fact, the bridge *followed* the first recruits to Sassaby. Experienced and talented cosmetics industry managers and technicians approached Sassaby and asked to be rescued from the uncertainty and turmoil of the merger situation. Within months, they had assembled the specific talent needed to run the business—sales and marketing, package engineering, quality assurance, purchasing, and production planning. In an intensely competitive cosmetics market where tiny start-ups are at best risky, Jane has been a stunning success. Within just three years, sales blossomed and Jane became the eighth largest mass-market color cosmetics line.

TALENT MAGNET

Your successful magnet strategy can and must reach far beyond attracting merger refugees. Your firm can become a magnet for the best employees from many sources, including the top business and engineering schools and other firms not mired in merger integration turmoil. The same qualities that make your company attractive to refugees will also make it attractive to many other talented technicians and managers. When your firm creates a reputation as an industry leader and "a great place to work that only hires the best people," you create a self-fulfilling prophecy. Top talent attracts talent. In every industry, the most talented managers act as magnets. Top talent comes running to grab at opportunities to work for you and you can handpick the best and brightest. Your sterling reputation is then further enhanced, and even more great candidates will knock at your door. This cycle goes on and on as you continually build your human resource capability, stronger competitive competencies, and greater management depth.

But you cannot become a magnet for top talent using smoke and mirrors. You must earn your reputation through your abilities for both operational and strategic excellence. It's far too elementary for us to say, "Get a good reputation." A top firm's reputation only happens when others see your demonstrated skill and ability to execute with excellence a range of vital current business processes and proven expert competencies. Your firm's reputation as a magnet for top talent is built from within but is bestowed upon you *by others looking from the outside.*

Building a strong talent magnet is accomplished through both the draw of your institution and its reputation and the draw created by charismatic and trusted leaders. Some firms possess both—like General Electric. GE has been referred to as "the best business school in the country" because of its ability to attract and develop star-quality managers. And with CEO Jack Welch's legendary fame as "America's best manager," GE can be highly selective about who it hires.

The talent magnet has long been a critical component for many top-shelf organizations. When Michael Eisner first joined Walt Disney he was a magnet for top talent leaving other firms. Lou Gerstner became a magnet when he joined IBM. In every field, this magnet of top talent can be seen. Because the University of Chicago has had far more Nobel Prize winners than any other school, it continually attracts top talent. Classical music, dance, and drama students throughout the world dream of a chance to study at New York's famed Juilliard School. Each year hundreds of prospective students apply for admission, but only a handful of the most talented are accepted. Motown Records in the 1960s and 1970s created the very same cachet—all the most gifted rhythm and blues singers and musicians longed for an opportunity for just one audition with Motown founder and owner Berry Gordy Jr. In over two decades at Motown, Gordy produced hit after hit by star after star. All the very best up-and-coming young performers were drawn to "Hitsville, U.S.A." and the talent magnet of Motown.

Many great leaders have become magnets in their own right. Lee

Iacocca drew scores of gifted managers from Ford and General Motors as he worked the miracle turnaround at Chrysler in the late 1970s. Many of the brightest computer designers and engineers worked at Apple Computer, then Pixar, and then Apple again just to stay with Steve Jobs. National Football League coach Bill Parcells shaped winning teams with the New York Giants, New England Patriots, and New York Jets through his ability to attract skillful players and assistant coaches who all wanted to be part of Parcells' building of yet another winner.

Great companies create a reputation that is very similar to the strongest brand loyalty for consumers. Graduate business students clamor for a chance to "build their career" with a McKinsey & Co. or a Goldman Sachs. These star firms offer more than just a job—they offer the deep pride and loyalty that employees develop while working for them. They become the employer of choice in their industry. GE, Merck, Intel, Citigroup, Toyota, Microsoft, Ford, Wal-Mart, and now new firms like Dell, Sun Microsystems, Oracle, America Online, Nokia, Cisco Systems, and global wireless king Vodaphone Group PLC/AirTouch Communications are magnets for top talent from many sources and their success breeds more and more success. As well-known magnets for the best talent, they will all continue to be formidable foes and fierce industry competitors for many years in the future.

This magnet strategy is not just one of several non-merger strategies you should have in your strategic toolkit. *It is essential.* Building your entire company into a magnet for top talent from multiple sources can be the most important factor in sharply improving and broadly enhancing many of your competitive advantages.

Your comprehensive magnet strategy is most effective when you weave the expectation for this strategy's successful achievement deeply throughout your organization. Just as most of General Electric's many businesses are each required to continually scan their industry and the world for the best acquisition targets, when you have many eyes aiming at the same target, you galvanize the entire firm into a higher gear. Companies that depend solely upon a human resource department to recruit and staff their operations are generally sorely disappointed. When many of your people are using their numerous external connections to mine for just the right talent to strengthen their own teams, your firm will attract far more gifted recruits while simultaneously keeping them from the grasp of your competitors.

Because mergers create fear, uncertainty, and anxiety among employees of both the acquiring and the target firms, you are presented with the perfect opportunity to launch your firm's magnet strategy in the least expensive and most strategically efficient way possible. Your company can simply open its arms to create a safe harbor for talented merger refugees, attracting key people who simultaneously build your strength, competitive competencies, and technical expertise while significantly weakening your competition when they are most vulnerable to losing forward momentum.

3

Attack When Competitors Are Distracted

There is another vital strategy noncombining firms use to exploit their merging competitors. You can time strategic attacks against your competitors precisely when those firms are most vulnerable—when they are floundering in the chaos of merger or acquisition integration. Integration can be so disruptive that combining firms lose at least part of their external vision because they are forced to focus inward on their immediate acquisition or merger integration problems. Your corporate attacks are most effective when they blindside competitors.

One classic example of this is Coca-Cola Co.'s acquisition and troubled management of Columbia Pictures Corporation, which gave PepsiCo's "Choice of a New Generation" marketing campaign just the boost it needed to be a huge success. Coke, struggling to find its way in the Columbia Pictures acquisition integration, saw its own legendary marketing organization flounder in response to Pepsi's bold advertising starring pop star Michael Jackson. Its response was to replace its traditional Coca-Cola with "New Coke"—which quickly became *one of the greatest marketing fiascoes of the century.* The public didn't like New Coke and wouldn't buy it. The firm finally reinstated Classic Coke and ultimately sold off their disastrous Columbia Pictures acquisition. Pepsi stole market share by attacking when Coke was most vulnerable and *outsold Coke for the very first time ever.*[1]

Even Pepsi's chairman and CEO Roger Enrico may have failed to recognize the gift Coke handed to him—at least he never mentioned it in his book, *The Other Guy Blinked.* He was convinced Pepsi's revolutionary advertising using—of all personalities—a frail, one-gloved pop star was the key to stealing market share from Coke. He was only *partially* correct. The other major cause of Pepsi's success was the self-imposed internal chaos and organizational drag at Coke as they struggled to digest Columbia Pictures. Pepsi's timing, intentional or not, could not have been more fortuitous.

Coke's management, which was so successful in the soft drink industry, quickly became a glaring liability as they struggled to integrate a motion picture studio. The mega-hit *Ghostbusters* was already in development when Coke bought Columbia in 1982. *Ghostbusters* was released in 1984 and quickly became a box office hit and financial success. But success didn't last long. The next Coke and Columbia big budget films were the highly forgettable *Ishtar* and *Leonard, Part 6.* Even with high profile stars like Dustin Hoffman, Warren Beatty, and Bill Cosby to draw moviegoers to the box office, both films were terrible flops. *Ishtar* continues to be included in many film critics' "Ten Worst Films of All Time" lists.

And while the Columbia division was bleeding, Coke was simultaneously creating the most famous marketing blunder ever. Their drastic response to Pepsi's growing market share was the ill-conceived "New" Coke. Even without reliable consumer research data, Coke replaced the most popular cola beverage of all time. New Coke lasted an embarrassing three months before "Old" Coke was brought back in response to the overwhelming outrage of loyal Coke drinkers. Coke's late CEO Roberto Goizueta's only regret was that he didn't bring back "Old" Coke in one month instead of three.[2] Coke had created marketing history—the very same company had simultaneously created *Ishtar* and "New" Coke!

Even for top-shelf companies like Coke, the impact of absorbing an acquisition can be devastating. For decades, banks, computer and automotive manufacturers, and other firms have launched aggressive new product or service introductions and marketing campaigns much more successfully when they were timed to coincide with their direct competitor's merger distractions. A company in the midst of a merger simply does not have the same ability to launch countermeasures while they are busy integrating staffs and operations. A poorly planned merger integration heaps so much extra work on managers that the company is simply *unable* to respond to attacks against its market share.

To further compound the gravitational pull caused by the typical merger or acquisition, when customers see their supplier in the midst of a troublesome integration, they know that uninterrupted and on-time deliveries can be in serious jeopardy. A business that lives or dies by the reliability of its vendors will listen to proposals for alternative supplier sources—like you. Airbus Industrie was able to steal business away from The Boeing Company in just this way. Boeing's internal problems resulting from simultaneously trying to integrate two newly purchased firms (McDonnell Douglas and Rockwell International's defense operations) caused them to miss delivery commitments—and Airbus knew it. (See Appendix E for details.) Their sales force used this critical fact to convince air carriers to place their next jetliner orders with Airbus. In fact, U.S. Airways and British Airways had *never* purchased airliners from Airbus until Boeing fumbled its merger integration. This approach helped Airbus win the majority of the globe's aircraft manufacturing business for the first time in their thirty year history. In the first six months of 1999, Airbus won 66 percent of all new aircraft orders in the world precisely because it aggressively attacked Boeing when it was still engulfed in the chaos of merger integration and massive production problems.

A golden opportunity to capture highly desirable suppliers is offered to your firm when your merging competitors delay or suddenly cancel orders. If the merging firms are in exact duplicate businesses, part of their planned cost synergies usually is to strip away duplicate inventories and cut back on suppliers. In the cases of typical merger chaos, where productivity actually shrinks to levels below those of pre-consolidation, total supplier orders also shrink. The merging firms often unmercifully jerk their suppliers, literally turning them on and off, as they struggle to meld their forecasting and production scheduling together. Good suppliers would much rather devote their capacity and attention to customers whose orders are predictable, without wild volume swings and false starts. Therefore, competitors' merger problems may well provide golden opportunities for you to forge new business relationships with a range of high-caliber suppliers on unusually favorable terms.

Union Pacific's ill-fated acquisition of Southern Pacific in 1997 shows how very vulnerable and distracted companies become when they bungle their merger integration. While trucking companies stole business away from Union Pacific, its rail customers, competitors, and government officials were calling for the dismantling of the ill-fated merger because of the absolute gridlock within the entire rail system that was caused by Union's and Southern's attempt to integrate their cars, tracks, and schedules. While officials at the Surface Transportation Board were trying to wade through the many options to solve the problem and revive the paralyzed railroads that stretched from the Gulf Coast to Southern California, Burlington Northern Santa Fe saw a golden opportunity. Burlington quickly crafted a masterpiece strategic attack that delivered a knock-out punch to Union Pacific.

Burlington was widely recognized within the industry as the only railroad with enough strength and resources to help resolve the Union Pacific rail disaster. It stepped in and proposed an unusual arrangement with Union. If Union would agree to share their track ownership and train dispatching, Burlington would *not* press for the breakup of the merger. Union Pacific had no better plan and because they were fearful that prolonging the gridlock would result in the Surface Transportation Board's potential undoing of the merger, they reluctantly agreed. They literally gave business to their main competitor as they were drowning in merger turmoil. In a classic demonstration of the double-edged sword, Burlington saw its financial results soar as Union's tumbled. At one point Burlington's net in-

Union Pacific vs. Burlington Northern

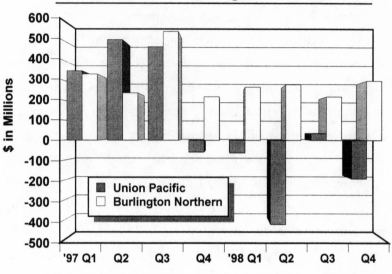

Source: Company Annual Reports

come jumped 77 percent while Union was quietly announcing their third straight quarterly loss.

Wal-Mart Stores Inc.'s greatest growth spurt in national discount retailing occurred while Sears, Roebuck & Co. was distracted by the two acquisitions it needed to build its short-lived Sears Financial Centers in the 1980s. In a move analysts called the "Stock and Socks" strategy, Sears was determined to offer its middle-class customers one-stop shopping for financial, insurance, and real estate services. It placed Sears Financial Centers in each of its department stores, with stock brokers and real estate agents right next to tires, car batteries, and wrenches. But the acquisitions of Dean Witter Reynolds and Coldwell Banker spelled disaster. Not that the expanded financial services were failures in their own right (the brokerage and real estate units were actually profitable), but the attempt to integrate these two mergers' processes stole critical top management time and blurred the vital organization focus Sears needed to win in the ever more competitive retailing industry. With Sears's attention diverted away from its core competency, Wal-Mart saw the perfect open door. Sears failed to see and understand the real threat of discount retailing as Wal-Mart began its insatiable U.S. expansion. Wal-Mart quickly snatched up the baton of retail leadership that Sears had dropped and ran away as Sears stood by helplessly. Sears had been the nation's leading retailer for generations, but they fell to number two and stayed there. In 1999 sales were $41 billion—just one-quarter of Wal-Mart's competition-destroying $165 billion.[3] Sears' financial services acquisitions caused it to lose retailing market leadership, forward momentum, and a sterling reputation that it has yet to recapture.

The recent demise of Al Dunlap's career at Sunbeam Corp. was the direct result of his simultaneous 1998 acquisition and fumbling of three different businesses—Coleman Co., First Alert, and Signature Brands. Dunlap was so preoccupied with his triple takeover that he made fatal sales, marketing, and operational blunders in Sunbeam's own businesses. Sunbeam's stock price was at a fifty-two-week high when he announced the acquisitions. In less than four months, it plunged over 84 percent. Sunbeam was a perfect target for strategic attacks.

Dunlap severely miscalculated the impact of simultaneously bringing together four previously separate companies. Sunbeam was already a bare bones operation due to Dunlap's slash-and-burn program executed in just seven months by early 1997. Before Dunlap, Sunbeam had been a $1 billion company with twelve thousand employees. Now it was a $1 billion company with six thousand em-

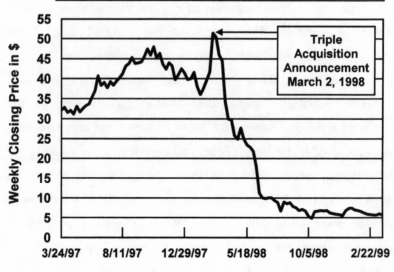

Sunbeam's Slide with Al Dunlap

Source: Yahoo!Finance

ployees. This skeleton crew could not successfully integrate the people, systems, and operations of three other newly acquired companies. The chaos finally exploded when Ron Perelman, a major Sunbeam shareholder, agreed to sell his huge majority stake in Coleman, and then squared off against Dunlap about how to best transition the Colemen acquisition. With total predictability, competitors reaped the benefits of Sunbeam's disorganization and infighting. Head-to-head rival and South Florida neighbor Windmere-Durable Holdings saw its share price rise to a fifty-two-week high during the very same four months Sunbeam's share price plummeted 84 percent. To add insult to injury, in *The Wall Street Journal's* annual Shareholder Scorecard, Sunbeam received the unenviable honor as the "Worst 1-Year Performer" for 1998. (See Appendix F for an expanded account of Dunlap's problems at Sunbeam.)

Whether your firm's competitive attacks are advertising campaigns, sales promotions, or the introduction of a new cluster of services, your noncombining firm must not miss the opportunity to initiate action while your competitor is merging. This will almost certainly mean moving timetables forward, but these time compressions will be worth far more financially than their incremental effort. When your head-to-head business initiative is timed to coincide with another firm's merger chaos, the initiative will produce better results because of your competitor's impaired ability to react.

Merger chaos doesn't discriminate based on company size, industry, or business sector. Small firms experience the same traps as their well-publicized giant corporate cousins. Merger distractions happen in every industry, even those that are long-established and presumably stable. Examples of business failures during merger distractions are virtually endless. The 1996 combination of Swiss pharmaceutical neighbors Ciba-Geigy Ltd. and Sandoz Ltd. to create Novartis AG, the world's second-ranking drug company behind only Glaxo Wellcome PLC, quickly resulted in market share erosion, as it fell behind both Merck & Co. and Johnson & Johnson. Airline industry upstart Southwest Airlines was able to quietly build itself into a national air carrier when American Airlines' parent AMR Corp. was distracted by its two-year-long "fake merger" alliance dance with British Airways and when both Northwest Airlines and Delta Air Lines were fighting over the right to merge with Continental Airlines.

Noncombining firms must not stand on the sidelines and passively watch the hectic merger activity around them. You must plan to execute a non-merger-based strategy by seizing golden opportunities away from your competitors. Therefore, your managers and teams must be constantly prepared to move fast to exploit competitors at the very moment they are most vulnerable. Your understanding of this rapidly weakening environment inside your merging competitor and knowing exactly when to best implement a strategy will help it succeed. You cannot afford to miss these golden gifts of your merging competitor's internal confusion, disorganization, and fear—they provide free fuel your firm can use to bound away from the grasp of market competitors.

4

Jump Start Vital Internal Changes

MICHAEL ARMSTRONG'S JUMP START

WorldCom Inc.'s sudden announcement of their $41 billion acquisition of MCI Communications Corp. in 1997 galvanized AT&T Corp. into aggressive action to change itself and radically improve its performance like nothing else had since the breakup of the old Ma Bell in 1984. A seismic shift was taking place in the U.S. and global telecom markets, and AT&T was falling seriously behind. AT&T's brand-new CEO Michael Armstrong used the WorldCom and MCI merger announcement to jump start the actions of the board, managers, and employees to immediately shift themselves into a higher gear.

Armstrong saw two critical factors: First, AT&T's cost structure was the most bloated in the industry. Over the years the organization's sales, general, and administrative (SG&A) expenses had ballooned to a distressing 29.8 percent of total revenue.[1] Second, up-start WorldCom's SG&A led all telecom companies with a slim 18 percent.[2] WorldCom had risen from virtually nowhere through their insatiable acquisition diet that culminated with the purchase of MCI, AT&T's main competitor.

Armstrong knew that WorldCom's stingy cost structure would be the standard for the merged companies. He had been with AT&T just ten days when the WorldCom/MCI deal was announced and he knew he had to strike quickly to mobilize his troops and undo AT&T's deeply imbedded spending habits. Armstrong could have stormed into AT&T and chain-sawed away forty thousand employees like an Al Dunlap. But with the stunning announcement of the WorldCom/MCI mega-merger, Armstrong knew he had the critical lever he needed to engage the entire organization in the race to drive out costs. This cost reduction program was not the personal whim of a new CEO trying to make his mark. It was a fight for survival against a formidable foe.

When Armstrong joined AT&T in November 1997, he knew he had to move fast to put the company into a competitive position so it would not miss out on the vast marketing and technology opportunities in the radically transforming telecommunications industry. Armstrong inherited a company that desperately needed deep-in-the-well, comprehensive change. *The Wall Street Journal* concluded that "AT&T's culture is focused too much on its past glory as the world's biggest telecom monopoly and not enough on the future, which would entail years of grim combat against SBC [Communications] and others."[3] Armstrong knew that he had to position AT&T more competitively at the intersection of the converging telephone,

Internet, and cable television industries. Additional cash resources were desperately needed to help fund acquisitions, joint ventures, strategic alliances, and technology upgrades. (In Chapter 7 we analyze in detail AT&T's numerous strategies for navigating in its hypercompetitive multimarket environment.) Armstrong wanted to save up to $5 billion each year by driving SG&A down to a more profit-enhancing 22 percent, where they could create a cost structure closer to leaner rivals such as WorldCom.[4]

Armstrong used a fast strike, "scatter bomb" attack on costs and inefficiencies—starting with senior executives. He streamlined the corporate decision-making process by consolidating several management policy committees into just one. Now top management decisions could be deployed to the organization within four days or less. And this was just the start of a series of changes for senior managers. Armstrong modified the management compensation plan so that up to 75 percent of a manager's total pay was tied to company financial performance. He eliminated company-provided limousines. He also required executives to vastly increase their ownership of AT&T stock.

Cost cutting cascaded down through the organization—Armstrong froze all hiring, offered voluntary separation packages in order to eliminate between fifteen thousand and eighteen thousand jobs, shut down unneeded facilities and ordered a 10 percent reduction in purchasing budgets. No component of AT&T's total cost structure was exempt from reduction or even elimination. His changes were broad-reaching and his cuts were swift and deep. But they were critical to AT&T's future viability against fierce, cutthroat competitors. Armstrong knew AT&T had to become lean—like

WorldCom. By using WorldCom's planned merger with MCI as the catalyst to jump start internal change, he gave AT&T a much needed wake-up call.

His jump-start strategy produced fast results. In one short year Armstrong was well on his way to transforming the once slow-moving, cumbersome long-distance giant into a svelte growth company at the leading edge of communications technology. Many opponents doubted Armstrong's ability to make AT&T into a leaner, more agile competitor, but investors knew better—by February 1999 AT&T's stock price was trading at an all-time high of $96 1/8. By the summer of 1999, total SG&A fell to 22.1 percent.[5]

Like Michael Armstrong at AT&T, you must use your firm's direct competitor's announcement of a merger, acquisition, major joint venture, or key strategic alliance to jump start vital internal changes in your company. Leading change is a challenge where few managers succeed. In-built bureaucracy, company-wide systems, and entrenched power structures actively resist change. However, your major direct competitor's merger or acquisition transforms your firm's competitive environment and that creates a daunting external challenge. You and your team need to use it as a major threat, a "trigger event" to initiate major changes throughout your company. *This is another golden non-merger opportunity you must not miss.* In short, this external threat can leverage your firm's entrenched bureaucracy to confront the urgent need to stop your old worst business practices or struggle forever in the tight grasp of the crowded field of market followers and lower-tier firms.

Here is your rallying cry: "Our major direct competitor's merger proves our industry is becoming much more intensely competitive.

We *must* all work together right now to make the necessary changes in company-wide cost reductions, revenue increases, and streamlined efficiencies to counter this new competitive threat. We cannot stand by and watch as our competition overwhelms us. We must change to improve how we work together in order to dramatically and quickly strengthen our competitive position. We *must* win this new battle."

Long gone are the days of blind obedience to managers' decrees. Now—more than ever—the better educated, more informed modern work force must analyze, understand, and internalize the need for lightning-quick change. They must be highly involved, accountable, and have a large measure of control over the change effort. When your employees have the same knowledge as you have about the changing competitive environment around your company, they will more readily embrace the need and urgency for change. An appeal to brace yourself for dramatically heightened competition against another nearly dominant firm is highly motivating and energizing to many employees. It calls out to a fundamental need—*the need to win.*

When your firm's competitors combine they may create an economic, technical, and financial force with such market power that, without your countermeasures, they can threaten your firm's very survival. If your people see and understand this threat they will more openly embrace needed change. Change is most effective when it has a defining event as a catalyst. Mergers or threats of mergers can be the perfect trigger event for many performance-enhancing changes. Whether your specific performance challenge is across-the-board cost reduction, increased productivity, improved quality, compressed time-to-market, or speeding the pace of innovation, your competitor's consolidation creates a critical rallying point for your firm. Whatever breakthrough changes are needed to place your company in a better competitive position can often be best sparked and fully activated by the sudden merger announcement of your direct competitors.

THE TOTAL TURNAROUND AT FORD

AT&T is not the only major company to use the consolidation of competitors to jump start internal change. Ford Motor Company's transformation into a world-class producer of quality cars stems from the direct threat of combining competitors. The past decade of success at Ford stands in stark contrast with their competitive position in the 1960s, 1970s, and early 1980s when the company was producing a full lineup of some of the world's worst cars. Seat-of-the-pants engineering, manufacturing rework, shoddy quality, and poor reliability ran rampant at Ford. During the three years beginning in 1980, operating losses totaled $3.26 billion.[6]

Although Ford had been exploring methods for turning around its ailing operations and income statement, it was the agreement of Toyota and General Motors Corp. to join forces and reopen GM's Fremont, California, assembly plant that immediately created an imposing double threat to Ford in the U.S. market. The joint venture was a marriage of convenience for both firms—GM wanted to learn the revered Toyota manufacturing system, which was the most productive in the entire automotive industry. Toyota, on the other hand, was on a scouting mission to learn how efficient American workers could become under Toyota's finely tuned management system.[7]

When GM's Fremont factory was shut down in 1982 and all the workers laid off, it was well known as the most inefficient of all GM's plants. When the plant was reopened in 1984, using the *very same* workers who had been laid off, sweeping new manufacturing practices were introduced by Toyota. The entire aged GM assembly process was scrapped and redesigned and what emerged was a U.S. model of the now-famous Toyota production system. Not only was it new, it was lean, fast, and cost effective. In its very first year it cut in *half* the days required to make each car and it would become the benchmark assembly plant within all of GM. Ford's chairman, Donald Petersen, knew his firm's viability was at stake, both from the threat of a number of vastly improved GM production plants, and from the imminent danger of Toyota setting up its own factories in the United States.

Petersen knew all too well that during the 1970s Ford had produced such "winners" as the Pinto and Zephyr. Pintos became infamous because of their deadly explosions in rear-end collisions. Don't be surprised if you can't recall the Zephyr—virtually all of them retired early into the nation's junkyards. Petersen immediately had to jump start radical internal change throughout Ford in order to compete in the domestic market against both GM and Toyota. Ford had to reverse its trend of shoddy craftsmanship because increasingly savvy customers expected and demanded much higher quality. The sudden Toyota/GM threat was the perfect high-octane trigger event to ignite Ford into action.

Through a fundamental transformation in its approach to work, fueled by the philosophies of W. Edwards Deming, Ford launched its famous "Quality is Job #1" initiative. They completely overhauled their design and engineering methods to attack process variability, manufacturing defects, and assembly line rework. The roles of managers and employees were totally redesigned to foster much more flexibility and autonomy within the work force. Ford drove decision making and authority down to shop-floor-level operating teams. They used multifunctional project teams to insure that design and manufacturing processes worked in tandem to build a high-quality, reliable vehicle at a competitive cost. Customer preferences were studied and understood so they could be integrated into each car. Ford succeeded in making the transition from a company-based definition of quality to a definition determined directly by their *customers*.

The first product of this entirely new system was the Taurus sedan in 1985. By 1992 the Taurus was the best-selling car in the United States and in 1993 Ford was producing five of the ten top-selling vehicles in the country.[8] No major company has reversed its reputation so completely and transformed its ability to produce high quality as dramatically as Ford Motor Company. The joint venture of Toyota and General Motors was the crucial external event Ford needed to drive sweeping internal changes throughout its entire world-wide organization where nothing else had succeeded in accomplishing this in the previous twenty years. Finally, Ford's transformation was clearly not a program of the month, but was a very real, *embedded* change—after five years Ford Motor Co. was still winning both the loyalty and pocketbooks of consumers, again selling five of the top ten vehicles in 1998.[9]

Ford was not the only car manufacturer to use competitor consolidations to jump start vital internal changes. As the twentieth century rolled to an end, the race for giant size accelerated even more. The automotive industry tightly embraced the narrow view that bigger is better. In fact, industry analysts proclaimed that a car maker must produce at least 4 million cars each year to remain viable in the truly global automotive business. Daimler-Benz and Chrysler merged. BMW bought (and later sold) Rover, and Renault SA acquired controlling interest in Nissan Motor Co. Even Ford acquired Volvo.

However, executives at both Honda Motor Co. and Toyota Motor Co. knew that if they copied the tunnel vision of the automotive companies merging all around them they would squander their resources, severely limit their strategic choices, and lose their ability to outpace competitors. Honda's president Hiroyuki Yoshino and Toyota's president Hiroshi Okuda both knew a panoramic view of all their strategic opportunities was key to their "go it alone" decision. Both men chose to remain off the M&A battlefield, but to gain competitive advantages by instituting internal change spawned by the threat posed by their merging competitors.

By the summer of 1999, both companies' internal plans were in place. Toyota chose to adopt the supply chain philosophy and model of Dell Computer, making each car to a customer order. Starting with the Camry Solara coupe, Toyota aimed to reduce each customer's order time to *just five days.* As the industry standard to produce a custom order typically required one to two months, five days became an immense challenge. But automotive supply-chain expert Jeffrey Bodenstab clearly understood the importance of Toyota's make-to-order undertaking. "By making and delivering personal computers to order, Dell Computer catapulted itself from a crowded field to become an industry leader."[10] The benefits of this drastic delivery time reduction are numerous. Toyota will save billions of dollars in inventory carrying costs all along its supply chain while winning new customers attracted to the convenience of quick delivery. This fast delivery builds repeat business and brand loyalty not only from individual consumers but also from major fleet purchase customers.

Other internal changes within Toyota produced its new "world-beater" Echo subcompact. Through engineering advances that shaved $2,600 off the price of the Tercel (the car Echo replaced), Toyota could still profit from a car it priced at just $9,995—fully 15 to 20 percent below comparable models from Detroit's "Big Three."

At Honda, the company-wide goal was to reduce the time and cost for new-model introductions by *50 percent* through standardizing assembly tools and building an entirely new, vastly more flexible and efficient manufacturing system. "Who says you have to be a member of the four million club to survive?" asked president Yoshino. "If you spend small, then you don't have to sell a lot to be profitable."[12]

The presidents of both Honda and Toyota challenged their firms with extremely aggressive goals that will only be reached through true organization-wide commitment and tremendous effort. Additionally, by focusing on critical internal changes, Toyota and Honda will take the lead in the global race to market a much more efficient and environmentally friendly car. Both companies introduced a hybrid gas and electric powered car in 2000. The Honda Insight and Toyota Prius deliver up to a stingy 70 miles per gallon of fuel. The old saying, "A new idea is born when two old ideas meet each other for the first time" was indeed embraced by both firms. By combining two established technologies, Honda and Toyota have won the fierce auto industry fight to provide a truly breakthrough "green" car. In the end, Honda and Toyota will solidify their standing as the most responsive, fastest, and most efficient car makers in the world—sources of competitive advantage that giant size alone can never achieve.

Consolidation is changing the competitive arena for virtually every industry. Even if your firm chooses to *not* combine with others, you cannot stand on the sidelines and simply watch the frenzy around you. Firms of all sizes from all industries will see ever-increasing consolidation activity around them. To remain competitive, every firm must continually make improvements to its internal operations. The external trigger event caused by the mergers or acquisitions of your competitors is the right time to initiate change at your firm. When you use this non-merger strategy, change can be implemented faster and with better results than a "born from within" improvement effort.

5

Key Merger Alternatives

Instead of paying excessive prices for acquisitions and exposing your company to the 80 percent probability of merger failure, consider some key alternatives to mergers—alliances, joint ventures, licensing networks and franchising. These alternatives are cheaper, faster, more flexible, and far easier to enter into and exit from than corporate acquisitions and mergers. Since no acquisition control price premium must be paid to enter merger alternatives, often they are financially less risky and provide far higher financial returns than a merger or acquisition. Not only is their rate of success higher than for mergers, but these vital alternative strategies *aim at targets that are easier to hit.*

Mergers and acquisitions are almost always an "all or nothing" proposition. They are not like shopping in your local grocery store—unless you can imagine being forced to buy every item in the store just to get the ones you want and need. Acquiring firms normally cannot shop exclusively for specific desired parts of a potential target. They must purchase the entire target—the desirable parts and also those that are not needed nor wanted. Many business units of a target company may not fit strategically, geographically, or financially with the acquirer, but they come with the package, often driving up the total acquisition price well beyond reasonable levels. While you can usually sell undesired pieces of a target business, you are often forced to accept less than market value because the world is fully aware that you didn't want that particular part of the target from the very start.

For decades, many governments around the globe prohibited foreign corporations' acquisitions of domestic firms, and many still do. Other governments put so many roadblocks, restrictions, and delays in the way of foreigners' acquisitions that they were uneconomic or led to failure. By contrast, it is far easier to get foreign governments' regulatory approvals for most strategic alliances, joint ventures, franchises, or licensing deals.

Strategic alliances are exploding in many industries—including e-commerce, communications, transportation, lodging, financial services, media, and computer industries. For example, airlines enter simultaneous multiple alliance agreements as the easiest, cheapest, fastest, or *only* possible way to expand their global or domestic reach for customers, to significantly lower their costs, or to gain access to slots, gates, routes, and airport lounges. The scope of many airline alliances has vastly expanded from co-marketing to include shared staff, flight equipment and computerized reservation systems.

Andersen Consulting predicts alliances will represent between $25 trillion and $40 trillion in value by 2005.[1] The explosive proliferation of alliances is driven by their speed of completion, more immediate cost savings, instant geographic expansion to new regions, and fewer approvals by governments or shareholders. Alliances present potent financial and business advantages which countless companies in many different countries have experienced already. Many more will do so. Strategic alliances between pharmaceutical giants, high-tech and biotech firms are now viewed as imperative.

You must not, however, confuse a pure alliance with contract outsourcing. Internet routing gear maker Cisco Systems created a highly responsive, quick time-to-market product supply system by contracting out a huge majority of its manufacturing and logistics to "electronic manufacturing service providers."Cisco has been able to capture a majority of its market, in part, because of this system. While Cisco has been successful using this model, outsourcing can become a double-edged sword—over time you risk losing your own critical core competencies.

Oracle Corporation alone has entered into almost 16,000 different alliances.[2] Strategic alliances span a very wide spectrum, from minimalist co-marketing of one product all the way to shared staffs, buildings, equipment, systems, operations, and customers—much like a merger. For example, two or three firms' brand images may appear on a plastic cup, as in McDonald's restaurants with its Golden Arches next to a picture of Walt Disney's Animal Kingdom theme park, next to the logo of Coca-Cola. Many different versions of this co-branding alliance between the three firms have lasted for over forty years. It's proved very useful to all three firms as they spread their separate operations steadily into ever more countries and new regions, continually leveraging off each firm's famous brand and well-known image in their new promotions. But their alliance was always limited. In contrast, the strategic alliance proposed between American Airlines and British Airways encompassed a near total sharing of stock ownership, equipment, crews, and operations. Their alliance structure looked like a disguised merger, so regulators withheld legal permissions for three years in attempt to resolve monopolization issues. The important point is that strategic alliances can be as narrow or broad as you wish, and can accomplish many of the goals of a merger with less cost.

Global alliances for cross-marketing drugs have long been common in the pharmaceutical industry, but now, most new emerging hypercompetitive industries are recognizing the value of strategic alliances and joint venture alternatives. When Yahoo! and MCI agreed to launch a co-branded Internet service provider, they quickly created a formidable challenge to America Online's market dominance. Using the combination of MCI's extensive Internet network and the top search service of Yahoo! their alliance created a highly attractive alternative to AOL for the 50 million new users who came to the Web in 1998, and far more in 1999.

While the 1980s and 1990s were probably best known as decades of huge mergers and acquisitions (which no doubt will continue), we agree with the 1997 forecast of Leo Hindery, at the time president of Tele-Communications Inc., that "The next few years will be years of alliances."[3] This is primarily because, by the year 2000, speed to market has become the most vital imperative in global enterprise. No firm, not even GE, GM, AT&T, Microsoft, DaimlerChrysler, Mitsubishi, or Intel can afford to acquire all of the companies whose technologies, skills, brands, customers, or geographic markets they need to immediately exploit for many business opportunities, nor do even these giants have the luxury of time to develop all those critical resources through their own internal "organic" growth. Giant firms and tiny startups alike know many valuable business opportunities may be lost forever unless they can form multitudes of simultaneous partnerships with firms now in possession of resources their teams need. Tiny Internet firms and virtual firms often *must* have numerous alliances because they lack resources of their own. Vast networks of alliances are essential for most growth firms in order to maximize their strengths by leveraging off both their own and all their partners' webs of resources. In fact, the "bricks and clicks" revolution has been driven largely by alliances. Traditional brick-and-mortar firms link with high-tech Web companies to create new ventures that quickly combine the best elements of both worlds. For example, Gateway Inc. has teamed with OfficeMax to become the sole PC vendor at each of OfficeMax's 1000 stores. Through this "store-within-a-store," Gateway PC shoppers get ample opportunity for hands-on trials before ordering their custom-built PC either at the store or via Gateway's Internet Web site.

STRATEGIC ALLIANCES CAN MULTIPLY GROWTH VIA "NETWORK EXTERNALITIES"

One merger may double or triple your firm's productive range, but in the very same time period needed to complete that one merger integration, you can enter *dozens* of strategic alliances, and leverage off the resources or customer bases of many firms far faster and at a fraction of the cost of a merger. The basic comparison between mergers and alliances as two growth models is the stark difference between very slow addition and very fast multiplication in terms of the total required costs, time, resources, and potential financial payoffs.

For example, The Star Alliance is a partnership of key international airlines including United Airlines, Lufthansa, SAS, Air Canada, Thai Air, Varig of Brazil, Ansett Australia, Air New Zealand, Austrian Airlines, Singapore Airlines, and All Nippon Airways. (Mexicana Airlines and British Midland Airlines are scheduled to join.) Each airline brings to the Star Alliance its hub-and-spokes networks, gates at strategically located airports, its fleets, crews, loyal customers, frequent flier clubs, famous brand names, lounges, computer reservation systems, financial resources, and national government allies. This vast network connects travelers to 654 destinations in 108 countries. Any airline that joins the Star Alliance may share all the preexisting hub-and-spokes networks of routes, customers, and resources of current members. The Star Alliance's huge bulk orders (economies of scale) mean that a new member airline's business benefits are instantly multiplied by their joint increased financial leverage over suppliers. Star Alliance can buy aircraft, jet fuel, maintenance, catering, hotel space, car rental, security, and computers at deep discounts. This does not simply translate into lower costs for the new member but a lower cost structure for *all* existing members of the entire alliance when strong members join.

The increase in the Alliance's total profitability is derived not only from cost savings, but from shared access to every member's customers, which increases the ability to maximize total "yield management" of all seats on every plane. The Star Alliance enables members jointly to maximize the revenue of each seat and every square foot of cargo space in each of their planes, up to the moment every jet takes off, by sharing all space availability information on seats and cargo through their interconnected computer systems. Altogether, the Alliance's network externalities multiply benefits to all members, and like interlocking spider webs, they continually branch out to new regions to capture new customers.

Many positive benefits of network externalities are also spread simultaneously to each customer. Each airline can provide its clients with a far greater range of potential routes, destinations, and extra benefits like seamless global ticketing, more frequent flier miles, special tours, discounts on foreign car rentals, vacation package deals with hotels and restaurants, and promotions for large savings at countless shopping outlets, service centers, entertainment sites, and sports events.

Obviously, all strategic alliances can't offer the multiple benefits to their members and their customers that the Star Alliance can, and a considerable number of alliances fail to work out. Nevertheless, on average, the financial and business benefits from strategic alliances far surpass those from mergers for they are easier to network, and many can take place simultaneously. Compare the total range of multiple benefits immediately available to a new member joining the Star Alliance with a recent dilemma faced by just one airline— American Airlines, in its merger with Reno Air. American, the second largest U.S. carrier, was forced into a service shutdown in early 1999 when union pilots staged a "sick-out" due to disagreements about how to integrate Reno's pilot pay structure into American's. Within just eight days, American was forced to cancel 6,700 flights.

The sick-out wiped out over $200 million in pretax earnings—exactly half of the profits for the quarter.[4]

In September 1999, Internet retailer Amazon.com announced the launch of zShops, a new Web site on-line mall that sells over five hundred thousand items from thousands of smaller merchants. While Amazon was already well-established as the Internet leader in books, videos, and compact disks (and had expanded into consumer electronics, toys, pharmaceuticals, pet supplies, groceries, auctions, and greeting cards), CEO Jeffrey Bezos knew Amazon's strategy to enter specific product markets by establishing e-commerce order processing—but then shipping products directly from Amazon's giant brick-and-mortar distribution centers—would severely limit the company's entry into many smaller markets. Amazon had become a hybrid Internet/traditional business. Bezos wanted lightning-fast, pure Internet strategy, and zShops was born.

By simultaneously creating alliances with thousands of niche product manufacturers and retailers, Amazon shared its twelve million online customers, sophisticated one-click payment system, and specialized product search engine with any mom-and-pop business that joined the huge zShops alliance. Merchants of any size could join by paying a small monthly fee and a small percentage of sales. Orders processed through the Web site were shipped directly from each seller. With virtually no capital investment, Amazon was able to secure a vast new revenue stream.

Even before zShops was announced, thirty thousand new items were being added each day. The day zShops was formally announced to the press, Amazon's stock price jumped 23 percent. In another stunning press release just one week later, Amazon announced plans to become one of the first e-commerce companies to sell its products through handheld wireless devices like 3Com Corporation's Internet-capable Palm VII. Warren Adams, the executive in charge of the "Amazon Anywhere" initiative, stated, "Last week, we announced our new zShops, which was about anything. This is about anywhere. Now our customers can have their shopping mall in their pockets instead of having to be at their desktop."[5] With the introduction of zShops, it became very clear why Wal-Mart had been so agitated in early 1999 when Amazon hired away several of Wal-Mart's key IT professionals. Wal-Mart knew the power of a pure Internet mall alliance.

SHARED INTELLECTUAL PROPERTY: STRATEGIC ALLIANCES AND JOINT VENTURES

The Blackstone Group, a cross-border mergers and acquisition investment banking boutique, became well known for its innovation in forging strategic alliances and joint ventures between foreign companies to share intellectual properties. These cross-border arrangements were done to reduce research and development expenses, split global marketing expenses, and lower per-unit production costs through larger volume economies of scale. However, the key benefit was the combined R&D teams, drug patents, brand names, and sales forces that could be exploited jointly and simultaneously in a patchwork quilt of dozens of companies around the globe.

Sanofi-Sterling

The Blackstone Group's first such cross-border alliance was achieved at the end of 1991 between Sanofi S.A., a leading European pharmaceutical supplier, and Sterling Drug, then a unit of Kodak Corporation in the United States. As stated by Thomas Malnight and Michael Yoshino in their Harvard Business School Case *The Blackstone Group*, "Previously, each firm alone had been smaller than the optimal size for being competitive in the pharmaceutical industry. Yet both possessed complementary product strengths. The deal was structured to keep their research activities independent, but designed to share product development expenses, combine marketing capabilities and split additional revenue, all in a tax efficient manner."[6] In mergers and acquisitions, there are often huge expenses, tax consequences, wrangling over control, delays in negotiations, and years of corporate integration problems. However, in the Blackstone Group's unique strategic alliance for Sanofi and Sterling, "(t)he transaction was structured in such a way that no cash, securities, or debt were exchanged, no existing earnings diluted, no assets transferred, or any taxes paid. The agreements were designed to maintain each firm's corporate identity and existing operations, while allowing increased cooperation on escalating R&D activities, a major challenge facing both companies."[7]

HIDDEN DANGERS AND GREAT RICHES OF STRATEGIC ALLIANCES

From 1970 to 1999, Japan's NEC Corp. entered into between one hundred and two hundred strategic alliances with many companies. "As they entered collaborative arrangements, NEC's operating managers understood the rationale for these alliances and the goal of internalizing partner skills," say C. K. Prahalad and Gary Hamel in their landmark article "The Core Competence of the Corporation."[8] In short, NEC and many other firms specifically set out to *exploit* all their strategic alliance partners. As one CEO explicitly directed his employees: "We must digest their skills."

Therefore, your firm's team must prepare itself before entering any strategic alliance in order to determine exactly what you intend to learn from your corporate partners and to plan how best to share in their whole range of resources and core competencies. Otherwise, it will be your firm that will be exploited by your strategic alliance partners.

Whereas Japanese firms all have a rigid "gatekeeper" for their joint ventures or strategic alliances to protect their own companies' secrets and to make the most efficient and concerted effort to extract knowledge from their foreign partners, most U.S. and Western firms have *not* used these gatekeepers. Thus, the American cultural habit of teaching and sharing knowledge created a huge leakage of the latest technology, know-how, various types of buyer preferences, and even thousands of specific customer lists. In contrast, there has been remarkably little reciprocal leakage of Japanese firms' know-how to their Western strategic alliance partners.

Therefore, your firm must always create a gatekeeper for all your strategic alliances and joint ventures, specifically to insure that accidental leakage of your firm's precious technology and know-how does not take place, and to make sure that your entire team sets out to learn as much as is humanly possible about your strategic alliance partners' operations, technologies, process know-how, and best practices. Your gatekeeper also must make sure to regularly collect all this information from your team members who are involved at any level in any strategic alliances with any other firms. Then your gate-keeper must quickly transmit all key information from your partners directly to each of your firm's managers, teams, or businesses that could benefit from this vital information.

For example, Motorola is by far the best U.S. corporation at using its own gatekeeper for making sure its entire team only very slowly released small amounts of key proprietary information to their Japanese alliance partners—and only *if, as, and when* Motorola won a specific target percentage of actual Japanese market share. By using their highly desirable proprietary information as a *reward* for market share, Motorola was able to win a huge percentage of the Japanese wireless phone market, which had been its key goal. Motorola used this same technology gatekeeper and foreign market share capture strategy in many other countries.

While thousands of strategic alliances make them the most common form of merger alternative, huge benefits can be derived from joint ventures, licensing deals, as well as various franchising structures. Each can be done separately, but in certain cases they are best used in combination, as we will analyze in Chapter 7. In many of these non-merger combining models there are significant financial benefits, plus nonfinancial advantages, which have become increasingly apparent to managers in a wide variety of industries. These non-merger alternatives often leverage off the partner firm's strengths, including its deep pockets, geographic market power, innovative technology, strong well-established reputation, service network, existing product distribution system, sophisticated customer and supplier information system, highly experienced managers and technical experts, its highly successful marketing formula, or access to low-cost debt. While these joint ventures and alliances can provide benefits similar to those that would have been sought in a full-scale acquisition, these benefits are usually obtained at a fraction of the cost, in much less time, with little or no governmental regulatory review, without the need for share-holder approval, and they are tailored specifically for the targeted pur-poses desired by both corporate parties.

Like alliances, licensing of technology, trademarks, or copyrights can drive corporate growth at an explosive pace. No contrast be-tween two companies' growth is more revealing than by comparing Microsoft Corporation and Apple Computer. Whereas Microsoft li-censed its technology to thousands of software developers in order to create new products, Apple refused to do so. Apple was so in-wardly focused and rigidly protective they missed the most incredi-ble opportunities for business growth in any industry ever. No firm could thrive alone in the computer revolution. Microsoft's global network of licenses and cross-licenses continues to grow exponen-tially while Apple suffered for many years in near-bankruptcy.

JOINT VENTURES AS A KEY TOOL OF GLOBAL CONSOLIDATION

For over three centuries, joint ventures between firms have driven accelerated corporate growth in sales, profit, and cash flow to enable quick capture of new markets or create a host of new products or services. Joint ventures were crucial to launch old sailing ships and trading firms, whaling fleets, joint stock companies, early factories, and in building canals, mines, and railroads.

Joint ventures are even more essential today because of the explosive rate of globalization with cross-border projects in every nation, off every shore, in every ocean, in outer space and in every communications wave length. Many giant global projects—like Egypt's Aswan Dam, the British-French Concord jet, TGV High Speed Rail, the Channel Tunnel, or Hong Kong's $20 billion new airport—would not have started had they not been first structured as joint ventures, teaming local and foreign firms with huge multinationals and governments into complex networks. One trillion dollars is being invested in multiple aircraft joint ventures, another trillion is being poured into power and energy company joint ventures, and over a trillion is launching global joint ventures in telephone, wireless, cable, and satellite systems, as titans across most nations' communications industries are clustering into competing teams.

Take just one joint venture: that of movie studios Paramount and Twentieth Century Fox to co-produce the blockbuster movie *Titanic*, which practically overnight became the biggest grossing movie ever, passing $1 billion in just three months. Since this film cost over $200 million to produce, a joint venture agreement was struck in order for the studios to share in both risks and returns. Yet the film industry has seen hundreds of joint ventures over more than three decades. Industry professionals and their bankers say this was inevitable, as the average cost of one big star in one film has risen to $20 million (often plus a percent of the gross receipts) and the total annual cost to run a studio is now between $2 billion and $4 billion.

Likewise, for seventy years giant oil companies have been forced to form joint ventures with other giants in order to afford the multibillion-dollar costs of worldwide deep-water, remote mountain, arctic, and desert oil exploration projects, while simultaneously managing thousands of miles of pipelines, off-shore drilling rigs, huge refining plants, tanker fleets, storage facilities, and networks of distribution systems within each nation. Not only do these joint ventures share huge costs, resources, and skills, but they have made possible many vast decade-long projects that politically, legally, and technologically, would be prohibitive for a single company. This is not to say that joint ventures always succeed, or are easy to manage, but in our economically complex, politically fragmented world, joint ventures have virtually always been permitted, while many mergers or acquisitions of those same firms would not. Even while Microsoft was losing its famous antitrust trial, it teamed with Andersen Consulting to create Avanade, a 5,000-employee Internet enterprises consulting company. Through this joint venture Microsoft immediately gained enough cutting-edge technical service muscle to compete toe-to-toe with IBM and Oracle for huge global e-commerce and technology jobs.

FRANCHISES: A FAST GROWTH ENGINE

One of the fastest growing business models in the world is the franchise, which in the United States alone accounts for about $1 trillion, *or fully one-half of all retail sales.*[9] This huge dollar total may be surprising, but just consider that most gas stations, car dealers, hotels, insurance brokers, real estate firms, and most drug, shoe, clothing, cosmetics, and hardware stores, along with tax preparation firms, local phone firms, fast food outlets, beauticians, temporary labor and cleaning services, are in fact structured and run as franchises. A franchise is a simple but very powerful business model that offers key advantages both to the franchise owner and to individual franchisees. By far the most important reason for franchise companies' rapid growth and huge financial impact is because each firm leverages its fast expansion directly off many other people's money, their direct investment, and continued funding, plus it leverages its growth off thousands of franchise owners' long hours and great efforts—their "sweat equity."

Ray Kroc who founded McDonald's fast food restaurants, the Pritzker family who emigrated from Russia and founded Hyatt Hotels, and England's Anita Roddick who founded the Body Shop Ltd. cosmetics store each did so with the *tiniest of their own resources.* In fact, their franchise business models all arose from necessity. Originally, none of them had enough of his or her own money to pay for the bricks and mortar to expand their businesses, nor were they originally sufficiently creditworthy to borrow the necessary capital for fast growth. If their start-up ventures were to survive and flourish, they had to convince other entrepreneurs to invest their own money and to devote huge personal effort to copy the founder's original model and start up their own fast food stores, hotels, or cosmetics shops.

Because the vast majority of new start-up entrepreneurs fail within the first five years, these three franchise pioneers knew what their strongest sales pitch to a prospective franchisee had to be: "Instead of trying to start a new business all alone and facing a very high probability of losing all your savings if your startup firm fails, you can become an entrepreneur with your own successful firm, right now, simply by copying our winning model business. We'll share with you all our secrets of how to make your new business work to quickly become successful. You are joining a partnership with us and with other franchisees to roll our new business concept across the U.S. or abroad. We teach you, train you, share your risks, and plan marketing for you in our pooled national advertisements. In return, we will take only a small fraction of the profit you will soon create with our model. You will be the business owner."

The power of the franchise business model is its financial leverage. For example, Mobil Oil Company has three types of gas stations. There are ones it built, owns, and manages, from which it earns 7 percent return on investment. Second, Mobil has gas stations it built and owned, but then franchised, on which it earns 14 percent ROI. Third, Mobil has thousands of franchisee gas stations which outside entrepreneurs paid for and run, on which Mobil earns a 24 percent return on its investment. By more than tripling its ROI on franchisees, Mobil, like all other franchise companies, is also multiplying its financial rate of return on assets, return on equity, and return on sales. That multiple enables many franchise owners to grow the business three times faster than a direct competitor who pays huge amounts to build and then manage networks of gas stations. The franchise owner must build, own, and successfully manage some of its own stores, hotels, or service businesses, in order to show potential franchisees exactly how to run one, and to keep innovating new improvements. Please note that the rates of return on franchisee versus company-owned stores can change significantly over time or in different regions, or for different products and services, in recessions or in saturated markets. Also, take note of the furious legal challenges confronting alleged abusive franchise owners by their franchisees. Courts now adjudicate in oversaturated territories.

Currently, GM, Ford, and Chrysler are buying back small franchised car dealerships to create larger regional giants which they will then refranchise. Coca-Cola and PepsiCo are doing similar buybacks of many bottlers to create giants—regionally, nationally, and globally—also to be refranchised. Parent companies in some of these cases retain a percent of ownership of the newly franchised businesses in order to dictate terms and retain a degree of future strategic direction. But they return to a super franchisee model to retain that great financial leverage of ROI, ROA, ROE, and ROS.

LICENSING, CROSS-LICENSING, INTELLECTUAL PROPERTY, AND SOCIAL CAPITAL ARE GROWTH ENGINES

Many of the world's fastest growing corporations are now referred to as "knowledge companies" because they leverage off the power of all employees' know-how, new processes, inventions, or new technology. *Intellectual property (IP) is the key asset of today's fastest growing firms,* not their physical assets like land, buildings, or equipment, nor their financial assets like cash. Soaring stock prices of many Internet companies, high-tech firms, and biotech outfits are not based on their ownership of bricks and mortar or cash balance. They stem from those firms' perceived intellectual capability to keep ahead of competitors through their ability to innovate, their unique technologies, and their brand names, customer loyalty, and global networks of allies. Many university sponsored "business incubator think tanks" have been established specifically to develop new IP.

The licensing and cross-licensing of all kinds of intellectual property like patents, trademarks, copyrights, know-how, process improvements, and loyal customer lists is one of the fastest growing fields in business. No firm, however large, exclusively owns all the re-

81

quired intellectual properties for continued financial success. As stated by the CEO of Japan's NEC Corp., "From an investment standpoint, it was much quicker and cheaper to use foreign technology. There wasn't a need for us to develop new ideas."[10] So, in order to speed up their own firms' growth, companies enter numerous licensing contracts with many firms simultaneously in order to gain access to the immensely valuable intellectual properties that will enable their firm to quickly expand its growth, size, geographic reach, or enhance its reputation. Large and small firms holding clusters of patents, copyrights, brand names, or process know-how increasingly must enter cross-licensing contracts in order to share in the pool of intellectual properties of other firms, whether they are partners or *even competitors.* Just as with alliances, your firm's ability to enter into many different IP licensing and cross-licensing contracts simultaneously will enable you to grow your business faster and cheaper than via expensive and time-consuming mergers or acquisitions. Finally, licensing and cross-licensing often have multiplicative growth benefits, for they are more easily networked together simultaneously with many other firms than is a typical corporate merger or acquisition. Because of the intensity of global competition it is becoming imperative for most firms to keep expanding their access to ever-newer intellectual properties. Thus, today's wave of intellectual property licensing and cross-licensing will increase significantly in the future.

Your firm can make an acquisition in order to own all the IP of another company, you can form joint ventures or strategic alliances to gain access—even temporary access—to specific types of intellectual properties. Alternatively, you can enter into contracts to license other firms' intellectual properties *right now* in order to capture current windows of opportunity around the globe. Carefully evaluate and select which of these strategies will provide your firm with the fastest growth, the cheapest cost, or the safest control of the collection of unique resources, intangible assets, or competencies that these intellectual properties may provide.

In the boldest and most aggressive strategic moves today, some firms rush to enter cross-licensing deals with other companies in order to share technologies they need immediately. They can't wait. Whether by voluntary deals, brute force, theft, or via use of strategic leverage, countless firms throughout the world now exploit each other's technologies or other intellectual properties. When giants cooperatively cross-license technologies, they multiply both firms' potential pool of future benefits, instantly expand the range of products each one could have achieved alone, and in so doing often leapfrog over competitors. In contrast, an indirect form of economic warfare has emerged in the guise of "patent flooding," in which a firm typically files for dozens of narrow patents closely related to a rival company's patent, literally boxing it in by building walls of patents around it. The targeted company finds it very difficult to improve its products or expand its market without infringing upon the flooder's patents, and is then often forced into exchanging or cross-licensing patent rights with the flooder. Finally, the growing global piracy of technologies together with many forms of intellectual property "leakage" via industrial espionage have become a legal and business nightmare. Nevertheless, all three of these examples of global licensing (voluntary, forced, or stolen) serve to emphasize how vitally important it is for growth businesses to share the IP resources of others.

In their book *Technology Licensing,* Russell Parr and Patrick Sullivan stress that "Interdependence is at the root of the paradigm shift taking place. Technology management in the future will center on leveraging technology that a company owns to gain access to technology that it needs. Sharing technology is a concept many will find difficult to accept, but accept it they must."[11] The strategic use of licensing and cross-licensing in today's consolidating world is a crucial tool for multiplying your growth. Whether you use IP licenses to enter alliances or joint ventures, to control your exclusivity, block another firm's growth, protect against competitors' innovations, or cross-license in order to obtain design freedom or for litigation avoidance, your company must analyze all these strategies. Otherwise, ruthless competitors will rapidly exploit your weakness in a stealth war against you. You must not ignore the power of these merger substitutes. They can provide the fuel you need to bound past your competitors—especially those mired in merger chaos.

All these key merger alternatives are growing as fast as, or in many cases far faster than, mergers or acquisitions. Their growth rates are driven by many of the forces that drive mergers—to reduce costs and to expand product range, global reach, market share, and profits. Yet the three key advantages these non-merger alternatives have over most acquisitions is their faster speed of implementation, target focus, and far greater range of access to business networks via cooperation.

Because of the three inherent powers of these merger alternatives, we tend to agree with the fundamental conclusion of Denis Waitley that "the leaders of present and future will be champions of cooperation more often than of competition."[12]

6

Implementing Fast-Track Combination

"Those who cannot remember the past are condemned to repeat it."

—George Santayana

There are times when a specific merger or acquisition is exactly the correct strategy to pursue as the crucial component to your firm's long-term financial success. Yet, if you choose to bring your firm onto the merger playing field, it is imperative for your team to plan and implement a fast-track integration—otherwise, your people will lose focus and your firm will join the 80 percent of all merging firms that fail to meet their financial objectives and erode shareholder wealth. (See Appendix G to learn about merger integration traps *individuals* fall prey to.) Without a skillfully planned and executed merger integration you will deliver the double-edged sword straight to your competitors and you will only watch from the sidelines as your industry's leaders race ahead. *Nothing can destroy your firm's competitive ability faster and as profoundly as a mismanaged merger integration.*

The typical merger or acquisition timeline simply moves the two

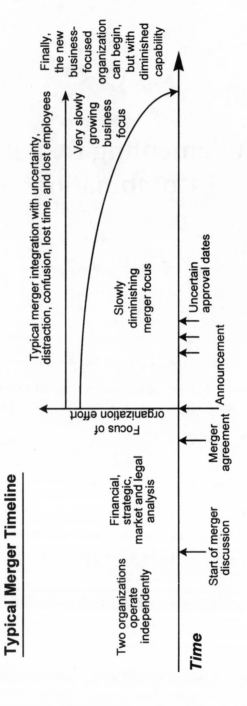

Typical **Merger Timeline**

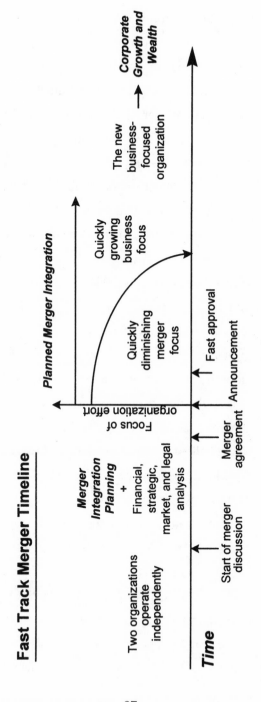

combining organizations through the integration far too slowly. Because the vast majority of firms do *no* merger integration planning, they have neither the skill nor the blueprint required to start the process with the needed velocity or to accelerate it in midstream. A 1997 Coopers & Lybrand merger study discovered a direct correlation between speed and merger success. They found a rapid transition increases the probability of achieving the merger's business objectives by 30 percent. Moreover, 89 percent of the firms in their survey believed they should have implemented an *even faster* integration.[1]

When Cisco Systems closed its acquisition of Cerent Corp. (just two months after the initial announcement), every Cerent employee already had a new Cisco job title, access to Cisco's Intranet, a boss, a bonus plan, and a health plan. Even before the announcement, Cisco mobilizes a transition SWAT team to insure the integration plan is carried out swiftly. The SWAT team works full-time to insure a fast integration and then updates its merger strategy procedure with new lessons so the next acquisition can be accomplished even faster and smoother. Cisco's lightning-fast integration process is a critical skill that will allow it to reach its target of twenty-five additional acquisitions in the last nine months of 2000 alone.

Your goal during merger integration is to move lightning fast, but in an organized manner. You almost cannot move *too* fast. Your organization must move through the time where it is focused on the merger integration *process* and into the time where your entire team's focus is squarely on achieving business *results*. Only then can your firm meet its financial goals. Everyone's participation is needed to insure the success of the merger. This maximizes the profitability of your merger because it minimizes wasted time, distractions, politics, and confusion that can cause delays in your combined businesses' forward momentum. The longer your firm's integration drags along, the deeper the hole from which the organization must climb.

Your newly merged firm must experience some kind of visible business success quickly. Starting with an action plan to achieve specific business milestones (such as three "easy wins" in the first six months) is usually the best way for your team to achieve joint success by the whole new organization. Winning must become an expectation and a way of life for your company because the downside risk of business failure is far too great. When organizations start their merger with failure, a battle over assigning blame and fault is inevitable. If you start with success and winning it will become contagious.

THE INTEGRATION CONTINUUM

The basic first step of your firm's successful fast-track integration is to determine exactly to what degree your two firms will be joined together. Acquiring organizations are normally in the driver's seat and they have many choices regarding the degree of integration with the target firm. At one extreme, your firm, as the acquirer, can take a "hands off" approach and develop a minimal connection between the two organizations. At the opposite extreme, the target firm's entire operations, systems, and people can be fully integrated with yours. Full integration requires your team to plan a comprehensive melding of your two firms' organizations, assets, systems, people, and various businesses.

The initial decision in any merger planning is to determine the depth of integration of the two former firms along the merger inte-

Merger Integration Continuum

←――――――――――――――――――――――――――→

Minimal Integration   Full Integration

gration continuum. The degree of integration you select can fall anywhere along this line. Nevertheless, your team must fully understand that with any chosen position along the continuum, success is
only possible using a fast-track timeline. The level of integration
must be very carefully deliberated. Far too many acquiring firms au-
tomatically assume the target firm will be fully assimilated into the
acquirer's operations. But many variables must be considered before
you make a wholesale jump into the potential fire of *full integration*.
The 80/20 principle provides a vital guideline when determining exactly how integrated your two former firms should become. Cisco's
acquisition success is in part due to the careful selection of business
functions that will remain *independent*. Cisco builds its success on
both speed and a minimalist approach to its level of merger integration.
If your team is careful to focus on 20 percent of the merger's required
integration actions that can drive 80 percent of your merger's total financial value and push your integration along on a fast-track schedule, you can dramatically increase the probability of merger success.

Minimal Integration

While the famous failures of the vast majority of totally unrelated
business conglomerates in the 1960s, '70s, and '80s have given minimalist corporate integration a bad reputation, in fact, a "hands off"
structure can be highly effective, profitable, and successful even
when a large number of combined firms are involved. Warren Buf-

fett's Berkshire Hathaway has achieved stunning success for over three decades. Merging firms can run as stand-alone businesses and then combine revenue and profits at the end of the accounting cycle. A minimalist merger integration is a key choice that you should consider *very* seriously because fully 50 percent of acquiring firms would have had *better* results if they had implemented this choice. Many acquirers are far too quick to jump into full integration without serious consideration of the infinite degrees of partial, tapered, or minimalist merger integration. This can be a costly mistake.

Jonathan Ledecky's U.S. Office Products Co. (USOP) is a classic example of minimalist integration during roll-up consolidation. (A roll-up is a quick consolidation of a highly fragmented industry.) After its IPO in January 1995, USOP made a weekly habit of acquiring local office supply companies, completing fifty-two acquisitions in 1996 alone. USOP targeted small, privately owned supply companies that had close relationships with office managers in local markets. They approached the supply company owners with a simple proposal—USOP would buy the company with USOP stock and cash. The owner always stayed in place. No personnel changes. No company name changes. No changes the customer could see. The only requirements were for the target to use the USOP financial system and to take full advantage of all the price discounts available through USOP's buying power with manufacturers.

Through a planned minimal integration, USOP achieved incredible results. Fiscal 1997 sales were up 305 percent to over $2.8 billion while net income soared 559 percent to $57.3 million.[2] USOP has not only proven the viability of the minimalist integration, they have achieved the elusive 2 + 2 = 5 synergy equation.

Compare USOP to another roll-up in exactly the same industry during the same timeframe. In 1996 Corporate Express, Inc. was even busier than USOP and became the most acquisitive company in the United States with an astonishing sixty-nine transactions. USOP and Corporate Express competed head-to-head as office supply consolidators. Their strategies were exact matches except for their level of merger integration. Corporate Express required target companies to adopt the Corporate Express name, employee uniforms, and other trappings that ultimately stripped the targets of their previous identities.

Despite what may seem trivial surface differences, the virtual hands-off approach of USOP delivered better business results. During the same time period, USOP's profit margin using the same roll-up strategy in the same industry was more than 58 percent better than Corporate Express's.[3] For roll-up consolidators in highly fragmented industries, the minimal integration should be seriously considered because it can produce better results.

While roll-ups normally crash as fast as they take off because "roll up artists" are normally financiers who lack in-depth industry expertise, the vital lesson gleaned from a direct comparison of USOP and Corporate Express is that minimal integration can actually help you increase the likelihood of a successful merger. By design, minimal integrations force you to focus on just those merger integration actions that will provide the very best contribution to the bottom line. Minimal integrations can protect you from attempting actions that only distract and confuse your new organization.

In early 1998 Ledecky broke USOP into five separate companies and moved on to focus on his two new roll-up ventures—U.S.A. Floral Products Inc. and Consolidation Capital Corp. Minimal integration will continue to provide Ledecky with a competitive advantage in his new endeavors. Ledecky's success in the office products roll-up provided Consolidation Capital a huge war chest to start another acquisition spree. Its IPO in 1997 had raised $480 million—*even before* Ledecky had announced which industry he would roll up.[4]

Full Integration

In full integration you meld together 100 percent of the two firm's systems, assets, practices, people, organization designs, and business units into one united organization. It is the choice of most acquirers and it is often entered into with little forethought about the organizational energy, focus, and total company-wide commitment required to make it successful. Investment bankers frequently provide the motivation for full integration by convincing acquiring companies that the wealth of overlapping and redundant operations, departments and systems will lead to easy cost reductions. But many managers think of merger integration as a simple "add on" to their core work and often push it aside or falsely assume it can be effectively accomplished by human resources department staffers. Boeing's traumatic integration with McDonnell Douglas fell victim to just this thinking. Full integration can only be accomplished on a fast-track schedule when it is carefully planned in advance of the merger announcement and integration start-up.

Moreover, your firm's decision to integrate fully must include an upfront determination as to the exact shape and composition of this full integration: Does it assume your target will adopt 100 percent of your firm's systems and best practices? Will full integration include a careful search, evaluation, and selection from the very best practices between the two former firms, or does it mean the firm's organizations will meet in the middle in an exercise of compromise? These questions must be answered by your team as the first key foundation stone for the level of integration determination. Your team, as the acquiring firm, must not make a blind assumption about the perceived superiority of all your firm's processes and systems over the best practices of the target firm. This simple but arrogant assumption can be a fatal trap and cause a cascade of serious mistakes.

THE FAST-TRACK SYSTEM

Effective integration only happens through the careful design and implementation of proven merger foundations and integration

Fast-Track Merger Framework

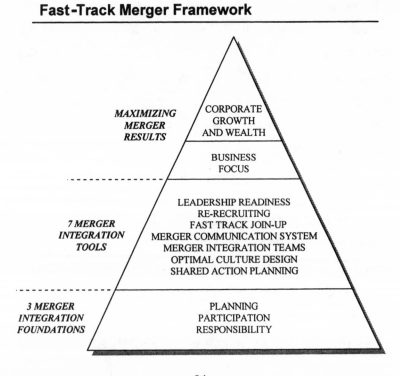

tools. Here we identify three foundations to guide your integration plan and decision making and seven merger integration tools to push your combined companies through the integration period quickly and into your new full business focus. Usually, only by following this type of plan can your team use fully integrated acquisitions or mergers to jump start your combined company's corporate growth and wealth.

MERGER INTEGRATION FOUNDATIONS

Three merger integration foundations should serve as guiding principles for your fast-track integration—planning, participation, and responsibility. When we look back at our detailed research into merger chaos and financial failure over five decades, in each instance we find a crucial foundation missing. Furthermore, merging firms that don't use one key foundation most often fail to use any of the three.

Merger integration must be planned in advance

Don't wait until after the deal is signed to start merger planning. *By then it is too late!* The die is cast. When polled *after* the merger, fully 80 percent of combining companies recognized planned merger integration as "very significant" to the success or failure of the merger.[5]

When Southwest Airlines acquired Morris Air in 1993, they studied the potential impact of the integration on personnel, equipment, flight schedules, and costs. From their studies they developed detailed plans for the integration. The final result? Their completed integration of Morris Air into Southwest's operations was accomplished in *just one-third the original timeline.*[6]

95

Broad participation throughout both organizations builds buy-in and commitment

Make sure members of both your organizations play an active role in your integration effort. Far too many merging firms fall into "victors" and "vanquished" roles. Only when the target company's best personnel participate in the integration is the acquisition done "with them" as opposed to being done "to them." The same holds true for your firm's members. Your team must be real partners with your target employees. No merger has ever succeeded where the combining parties just look to their counterparts in the other former firm to make the merger work. You must build a *real team* from the very start.

Participation of all key individuals involved in the integration from both former firms creates the best chance of true long-term internalization, acceptance, and real commitment. Success comes only when members of both your acquiring firm and your target drop their singular allegiance to their former companies and become advocates of your new combined organization.

Effective integration is every manager's responsibility

Starting with your initial merger announcement and ending with your combined organization, make sure everyone is aligned, and actually working toward common business objectives. In short, *every* manager in your firm and in your target must be truly proactively involved in the merger integration, and you must hold each one personally accountable for its success. When managers look to others to make the integration work, they are deflecting their own responsibility. As one Disney executive said regarding the rocky integration of Capital Cities/ABC, "ABC simply has to learn to adapt to Disney's procedural culture."[7] This executive points out how Disney was its own worst enemy and caused the merger to fail. By acting as "totalitarian dictators" to ABC, Disney top management spurred most top ABC managers immediately to jump ship.

Your firm's successful integration efforts must be always firmly anchored with the three merger integration foundations. When combining companies do not meet their revenue, profit, or value objectives (in the absence of excessive control price premiums), or experience culture clash, one of these foundations is usually missing.

Daimler's Merger Planning Approach

Daimler-Benz AG's 1998 acquisition of Chrysler Corp. is a useful example of using fast-track merger foundations. In fact, Daimler's acquisition planning started three years before any dealing for Chrysler started. In 1995 Chairman Juergen Schrempp ordered the construction of a "War Room," a high-tech command center outfitted with state-of-the-art communications technology. It was the link to strategic sites throughout the world, including Detroit, New York, and Tokyo. Schrempp also wanted Daimler to be ready with an "Integration Room," regardless of which firm became their merger partner. Most firms either wholly ignore the need for similar high-tech communication facilities, or else they do not plan their construction until after the deal has been signed. Schrempp knew that having his communication and integration rooms ready in advance would help to accomplish a fast-track integration when a merger partner was found, so he was ready three years in advance.

Schrempp and Chrysler CEO Robert Eaton had also created a detailed plan for the level of merger integration. They saw that key cost savings opportunities would come from finance and purchasing, along with support areas such as information technology and human resources. These areas became the focus of merger integration. Because each of the main business operations had already developed a great deal of momentum on its own, Schrempp and Eaton *decided to allow them to run as independent operations.* They knew that a full integration was not the best goal for DaimlerChrysler. Using the 80/20 principle, they placed DaimlerChrysler at the very strongest midway location along the integration continuum to yield the best financial results. The co-CEOs knew which integration activities would create the most value for both the company and it shareholders, and that is exactly where they directed the new organization's efforts.

In theory, members of both Daimler and Chrysler immediately became equal partners in the merger, starting with Schrempp and Eaton. Many CEOs share the chief executive responsibility because they cannot or will not agree who is the best to lead the new firm. That compromise often results from fear and suspicion. Schrempp and Eaton, however, chose the co-CEO format by a design to help the integration. Both men knew of the additional challenges of cross-continent mergers—national identities, diverse cultural norms, and different languages could all add to the difficulty of achieving a successful outcome. They were determined to establish an example of collaboration and cooperation, with neither firm taking a secondary role to the other. Because participation by both firms was key to merger success, they also created an executive integration committee that had equal membership from both firms and was led by Chrysler president Thomas Stallkemp.

Finally, Schrempp and Eaton made it exceedingly clear who was responsible for the winning merger. Together, they drove home their expectations in the very first meeting of the forty-manager lead integration team. As *The Wall Street Journal* reported, Juergen Schrempp and Robert Eaton presented each of those forty team members with a single certificate of DaimlerChrysler stock that was cut in half and framed. "You've got two years to make the merger a success," the managers were told. "If you succeed, you get the other half of your share. Of course if you don't deliver," the message continued ominously, "we will keep the other half. And that could be a problem."[8] Schrempp and Eaton knew just how essential it was for them to establish clear accountability. Their framed stock certificate reminders left absolutely no doubt in the minds of managers as to their collective responsibility for making the merger succeed. But DaimlerChrysler still faced huge problems.

MERGER INTEGRATION TOOLS

Seven merger integration tools constitute a proven method to ensure the three foundations are interwoven into integration planning, decision making, and implementation. These tools make up your merger integration toolkit. Like a carpenter, your team must select and use the best tool to meet each specific need. There is no single, magic "one size fits all" merger success equation; you must learn how each tool is used and then select the right mix of tools to best accomplish your firm's unique merger or acquisition integration.

Tool 1: Leadership Readiness

The lack of leadership readiness can be devastating to a merger integration—leaders own the implementation of a successful integration because they become the focal point of the organization after the merger announcement. Employees of both firms look to their leaders to learn what are the acceptable or expected actions as the companies join together. Top leaders must become key role models for the teamwork behaviors they expect from all others.

Your firm's leadership readiness also includes your preparation for the integration through establishing a successful framework like the one described in this chapter. Only then can your managers best participate in both planning and implementation. Additionally, learning about the many causes of past merger failures helps create a highly practical mindset for approaching the merger. In most unsuccessful acquisitions, George Santayana's famous aphorism becomes especially poignant: "Those who cannot remember the past are condemned to repeat it." This statement is especially true on your firm's merger and acquisition battlefield.

Tool 2: Re-recruiting

You must take aggressive steps to ensure that key results producers of the target firm do not leave your new organization. As we noted in Chapter 2's discussion of the magnet strategy, headhunters are on the prowl. They prey on your target employees' fear and uncertainty, and they target the very best performers and rob your new organization of the talent you need most to make the new merger work.

The very act of an acquisition radically transforms the mindset of target employees. When people seek employment, they normally experience a ritual typical in virtually every firm. They are screened, interviewed, tested, and, if they pass all the hurdles, are offered employment. They, in turn, either accept or decline. This process happens millions of times each year. But this is more than a simple transaction to match employers and employees, it is a critical ritual that creates a psychological contract. Your implicit contract is far more valuable than any legal employment document. Your team establishes the basis for mutual interdependence, trust, and faith. You must create a real bond.

In any acquisition, target employees are thrown into a mental tailspin because their critical psychological contract is breached. They feel as if they are simply another physical asset of the transaction and easily dispensable. If your firm fails to move quickly to reestablish an "I choose you, you choose me" bond, you foolishly risk losing the very talent your team needs to insure your merger's success. When Disney acquired Capital Cities/ABC in 1995 for $19.5 billion, their arrogance, ignorance, and insensitivity caused them to quickly lose the heads of ABC Sports, Research and Marketing, the Station Group, the Multimedia Group, and ABC Radio.[9] ABC television lost key executives so quickly that it plummeted from first place to third among the major networks.[10] Disney fumbled the job of re-recruiting their ABC team and severely diminished their capability to make the merger a success. A full three years after the merger, ABC was still listlessly floating in the number three spot behind NBC and CBS.

Tool 3: Fast-Track Join-Up

Even without special measures, merging organizations will learn about one another over time—but *too much time*. Merging companies must jump start the "getting to know you" process because, if it is allowed to evolve on its own, misinformation from the grapevine takes over and makes an effective join-up virtually unmanageable and extremely time consuming. The join-up is a planned, partnered, high-octane discovery process. It is used to expose, explore, share, and learn each firm's formal systems and design, their approaches for accomplishing work, and the differences between the two cultures. Merging firms do not intuitively know and understand what specific issues are potential integration traps that will cause conflict and infighting. They must force the discovery of potential conflicts before they create walls and battle lines between firms.

Your firm's join-up is a critical early step in your merger's successful integration. From business entertainment norms to organization structure to benefit programs to the pace of change, your combining organizations must learn about one another quickly in order to expose potential integration obstacles. Early in the Bankers Trust/Alex Brown integration the total lack of a rapid-fire join-up fueled bitter resentment and anxiety between the firms. For instance, Alex Brown managers were always expected to make decisions for their own areas of responsibility. On the other hand, Bankers Trust used consensus decision making, and to Alex Brown employees this decision technique looked like corporate-wide managerial indecisiveness. Alex Brown's culture frowned upon any dress other than formal business attire, while Bankers Trust enjoyed casual Fridays. Even well-intentioned celebrations caused controversy. After one dinner for partners and their spouses, the evening's entertainment was provided by the cast of the Broadway musical "High Society." Bankers Trust was doing its best to thank the partners, but Alex Brown executives scoffed that the show was excessive and wasteful.[11]

The triple merger of Bankers Trust, Alex Brown, and Deutsche Bank—creating what was at the time the world's largest financial institution with over $1 trillion in total assets—has continued to demonstrate how seemingly trivial issues can quickly create friction between merging firms. Adding Deutsche Bank to the mix further complicated an already difficult situation. Bankers Trust has been well-known for its freewheeling style. But soon after Deutsche Bank's acquisition of Bankers Trust, Chairman Rolf Breuer announced *during a press conference* that Deutsche Bank would put a tight rein on Bankers Trust. "We don't believe in autonomy. We will continue with our centralized management, so there will be no autonomy."[12] Immediately, Bankers Trust employees put his words on a large poster on their giant trading floor: THERE WILL BE NO AUTONOMY. Breuer's words soon began to haunt him as mass resignations started. These completely different cultures at the three firms exacerbated tensions and frictions in every stage of their merger process, which seriously undermined any semblance of an effective join-up to jump start the "getting to know you" process. When serious differences are discovered through the join-up, the firms must then work together to decide exactly which differences will be resolved in order to push the integration along and which will be left alone.

Tool 4: Merger Communication System

Timely, accurate information is essential to build trust and to move your combining organizations toward a business-focused environment at a faster pace. Misinformation and rumor mills are devastating to effective integration because they diffuse your organization's focus and can force the entire process to a grinding halt. The merger communication system isn't a simplistic "communicate, communicate, then communicate some more" tool. It is an organization-wide system to root out and pull merger questions and many negative concerns from the rumor mill before they can become festering wounds within your new organization. It allows your leaders to act forcefully to resolve conflict, issues, and worries. Without it, your people are constantly forced into a reactive backpedaling mode for resolving merger integration problems.

Your merger communication system creates an integrated organization-wide network of key people throughout all your teams, departments, and divisions who are assigned the role of "merger communication contact." They become the vital information conduits between their natural work group and both firms' merger leaders. They are responsible for an upward channeling of the concerns, fears, and questions of their co-workers, making it possible for your executives to learn quickly about integration problems and barriers.

Once armed with the issues that really matter to the merging organization, your leaders can then respond with the right information or make appropriate changes. But your leaders only earn the trust of the merging organization when they confront and resolve thorny issues head on. The merger communication system allows your leaders to pinpoint painful critical issues deep within your entire organization and then—through a multiple-channel communication return loop—to address employee fears and concerns. *Overcommunication is impossible* during your merger, so your leaders must use all available means, including company newspapers, live "town meetings," e-mail, video, or multiple small group question-and-answer sessions to keep communication channels open. The number one complaint of employees during hundreds of actual merger integrations was their lack of accurate information. Cisco uses on-going question-and-answer meetings specifically designed to reduce employee fear so they can focus on their work. False rumors and inaccuracies quickly spread throughout dual grapevines of the two formerly separate organizations. Therefore, it is vital for your entire merger team to realize that keeping people in the dark only fans the flames of fear and uncertainty. Your communication system must keep the accurate merger information flow wide open and frequent.

Tool 5: Merger Integration Teams

Any merger or acquisition can produce overlapping, redundant, or conflicting organization design components, systems, procedures, policies, or roles. Many managers have believed they could throw the merging firms into one blender, press "mix," and out would come a fully integrated, homogeneous new organization. *Nothing could be further from the truth.* Every merger, even those leaning toward minimal integration, will have a need to integrate various components of the combining businesses. The further along the integration continuum your firm ventures toward full integration, the more components you will need to integrate. This holds true even if you believe the two firms are "similar." Too many managers have fallen into the trap of discounting the need for integration teams because they believed the companies were much the same in terms of values, processes, and systems. Only after conflict and chaos erupt do they fully understand their shortsighted mistake.

Your firm's merger integration team is the essential tool to ensure the smoothest transition as your two firms meld their chosen business components into one. Such teams can serve a wide variety of roles. Any system, process, organization design element, or cultural component that could be a source of merger integration conflict must be addressed and resolved by a properly chartered integration team. Several dimensions are involved in this chartering process: Your team must include trusted managers from both organizations and key employees from the affected operational areas. Expected outcomes must be clearly described and the team's decision space precisely defined—exactly what are the boundaries (including time, resources, and authority) the team must observe? Finally, proper chartering of your team's goals and milestones always spells out very real accountability for your team's performance.

Depending on your chosen position along the merger integration continuum, you may have one or two teams or you may have many. If you plan a more comprehensive integration you will obviously need more teams. When you have multiple teams, each with a relatively small portion of the integration work, you gain two distinct merger integration advantages. First, you spread—and in fact multiply—the ranks of your people who can rightfully claim ownership of the successful merger throughout your organization. As participation increases you create a groundswell of motivation and accountability to make the merger work. Second, when many people are directly involved in the integration work, your firm moves through the merger integration-focused period much faster. When you move more quickly to the business-focused environment, the probability of merger success, quicker profitability, and forward momentum can soar.

What are the total consequences to your firm when the overlaps, conflicts, or duplications of the two separate businesses are not addressed and resolved? The harsh reality is that top-shelf firms and industry leaders can be brought to their knees. The total rail service meltdown at Union Pacific and Southern Pacific could have been prevented through careful planning and execution via intensely proactive integration teams. Pharmacia & Upjohn's two years of bitter internal feuding and poor financial performance could have been avoided. Any firm that enters into a merger integration without a plan to resolve the numerous sources of differences and serious potential conflicts will be duly rewarded with merger chaos and confusion.

Tool 6: Optimal Culture Design

For firms with generous amounts of self-confidence, a merger or acquisition is the perfect trigger event to create change in a current culture. Every organization has components of its corporate personality that could be improved or eliminated.

In 1989, giant Swiss Bank Corporation (SBC) was well known for its old-fashioned bankers and their deeply embedded stodginess. SBC, the weakest among the three largest Swiss banks, desperately wanted to become a major player in global banking. They wanted to globalize through acquisitions, however they knew their stodgy reputation for old-fashioned practices would only hinder them.

So CEO Marcel Ospel used the acquisition of the tiny Chicago derivatives boutique O'Connor Partners as the perfect catalyst to change SBC's own culture. O'Connor had earned a reputation as a group of young, aggressive, technology-savvy upstarts, so SBC adopted much of O'Connor's fast, flexible, aggressive culture in order to transform itself into a financial powerhouse for the twenty-first century.[13] To do this, they selected the best and most dynamic components of O'Connor's personality and directly incorporated each one into SBC through optimal culture design during merger integration.

Optimal culture design is most certainly not for every merger situation. In any merger or acquisition, a new, previously nonexistent culture will emerge. Even the most dominating, overbearing, deeply ingrained cultures of large organizations change, albeit slightly, when they acquire any target. This optimal culture design tool should only be deployed when a company truly recognizes that an improved corporate culture would be a real source of competitive advantage. They must also acknowledge that characteristics of their current culture need to be changed or eliminated. They must have copious amounts of self-assurance in order to make the meaningful effort that is absolutely necessary if the combined firm's culture is to be made stronger and more dynamic.

For seven years SBC succeeded through their optimal culture design. Their new-found dynamism was key to their rapid acquisition of SG Warburg in London, Dillon Read in the United States, and finally their much larger Swiss arch-rival UBS. Whether this giant multimerger, known as the New UBS, will be able to continue to build their optimal culture design, however, remains an open question.

Tool 7: Shared Action Planning

The ultimate, final goal of your firm's well-planned and executed merger integration process is to move quickly through the time when your organization effort is focused on merger issues and into the time where your effort is 100 percent devoted to delivering business results for your new organization. You will know when the integration work is complete and your new organization has emerged. No "we-they" conflicts. No lingering closets full of remaining integration issues. No constant fear of job security or changing responsibilities due to the merger.

In order for your organization to move quickly through the merger-focused time and into your business-focused phase, your new organization must have a unified approach for formulating strategies and developing plans to accomplish work within each area of responsibility. Otherwise, disunity will totally undermine all of your combined organization's strategies. This vital unification work is a normal part of the merger integration team's chartering process very early in the integration.

It is of such paramount importance for your team to have a unified approach for planning and accomplishing work, we are compelled to spell out this integration work as a completely separate tool. Too many merging firms lack the ability to develop strong strategic and operational plans—they just drift. Your firm's shared action planning tool must focus a vital part of your merger integration work on creating, building, and continually improving this profoundly important skill—achieving targeted quick and easy positive results.

For example, DaimlerChrysler began with a group of tiny successes to jump start winning as a way of life. By coordinating a series of changes, all scheduled to happen simultaneously on "Day One" for the new company, employees got their first taste of working and winning together. Through a well-orchestrated global effort, Day One marked the official birth of DaimlerChrysler. Every computer started up that day with the message "Welcome to Daimler-Chrysler. The future starts today." Each of the 428,000 employees received a letter from the co-chairmen, the first edition of the new company newsletter, and a watch with the new company logo. The

109

company Web page was inaugurated. The new DaimlerChrysler stock opened on both the New York and Frankfurt stock exchanges. Print advertising with photographs of pairs of employees broke in newspapers across both Germany and the United States. While these changes may seem trivial, they took true global coordination. Not only did they collectively boldly announce the arrival of DaimlerChrysler, they gave employees their first chance to work together. When the above-mentioned changes and a host of others all came together on Day One, a sense of accomplishment permeated the organization. This established a launching pad for the already planned ninty-nine "Synergy Projects"—all targeted to reduce costs or increase revenue.

When your organization basks in the feeling of business success, even if it is in many small improvements, both during and after the integration work, your probability of continued success is greatly enhanced. Creating a series of quick successes by your newly combined team, even if they are initially only small in dollar value, is how your merging firms win in the consolidating world—by delivering the right business results to lift sales, profits, and shareholder wealth.

THE FATAL COOKIE CUTTER

David McCourt, CEO of RNC Corporation, a New Jersey provider of communications services, recently stated, "Success breeds success formulas; success formulas breed failure."[14] While McCourt's statement covers immense territory, it reflects the experience of firms that conduct merger integration without a deep appreciation of the uniqueness of each integration. You must not assume a static world—the level of merger integration and the specific mix of integration tools used in one merger or acquisition will not guarantee an equation to be applied in all future combinations. Firms that adopt a static "success formula" will not be able to replicate past successes.

Sandy Weill at Citigroup learned just such a difficult lesson. Weill has been well-known as a savvy acquirer, buying or assuming control of mismanaged firms like Commercial Credit Corp., Primeamerica and Travelers. But when his Travelers acquired Citicorp (to form Citigroup) for almost $73 billion in 1998, Weill's standard approach backfired. Citicorp's CEO John Reed was a very capable executive, and his company was certainly not mismanaged. Weill's rough and tumble, take-control style led to what nine months after the merger announcement *Fortune* magazine labeled a "case study of trouble" in Citigroup's corporate business unit. This new firm's organizational structure was "terminally dysfunctional," and so the cookie cutter merger success formula that Sandy Weill had used for thirty years initially failed.[15]

Swiss Bank Corp. traveled a similar path of misfortune when it acquired UBS. While it had successfully integrated O'Connor Partners, SG Warburg, and Dillon Reed, Swiss Bank's formula quickly became a glaring liability with UBS. Its previous acquisitions had all been much smaller firms. But UBS was even larger than Swiss Bank and UBS employees were deeply entrenched in their bureaucracy— Swiss Bank's style was neither appreciated nor accepted. The battle lines became so clearly drawn that the new enormous organization became paralyzed with inaction. Young executives based in New York were even known to leave their offices to go to afternoon movies rather than be subjected to the abusive infighting and business paralysis the two firms were experiencing.

Your firm's successful merger integration will *only* happen on a fast-track schedule using the merger foundations and the right mix of merger tools. Remember, however, that like any skilled craftsman, you must use your tools in the proper manner and for the right application. Each merger situation is a unique event with its own hurdles, issues, and needs. You must treat each one as an individual case, use your tools to best address the situation on a fast-track schedule, and your merger integration will be a success. When your merger or acquisition succeeds and those of your competitors result in chaos, you gain a double advantage. Their forward momentum slams to a halt while your newly combined firm can race ahead, leaving them to suffer as market also-rans.

7

Composite Strategies to Match Your Complex Competitive Environment

Leapfrogging technologies and converging industries produce intensely competitive arenas that create many ways to lose, but just a few ways to win. You cannot expect to succeed in the future global business environment with only a single strategy. No firm is exempt from the impact of changing multiple competitors, markets, and technologies. A single strategy that may have succeeded for decades in the sleepy protected age of business in the past normally *cannot* create the best competitive positioning for your firm as it enters the global business arena of the future.

A composite strategy is no longer just an option—it is a strategic imperative that many firms *must* adopt in order to sprint past direct competitors. In fact, just to keep pace with the accelerating momentum of change resulting from today's rapidly consolidating industries requires ever-increasing flexibility. A composite strategy created from the simultaneous use of two or more of our first five strategies is key to your strategic agility and flexibility.

You must not, however, confuse an effective composite strategy with one that simply throws our array of strategic choices into a blender and then presses "mix." Historically, most firms that attempted to mix two or more strategies ultimately failed in both—they fell between two stools. They mixed together key strategies that could only succeed when they simultaneously hit *different* targets. Firms like General Motors—with too many brands—often corrupt dual, triple, or multiple strategies by allowing managers to aim them all at the very same strategic target, because they are unsure of how best to attack the specific target at the outset. Unfortunately, the consolidating world today is brutal and is far too complex for either such confused or overly elementary approaches. It is only mastered when your strategy is flexible enough to match rapidly converging industries, both in speed and multidimensionalism. A panoramic perspective is imperative today. You must be able to view the world through a high-power telescope while still being able to identify the minutiae of details visible only through a microscope.

Your firm's composite strategy must not be static or rigid. It is a dynamic, evolving process. Global Internet game theory provides a piercing analogy: Imagine a fiercely competitive game where you must play offense and defense at the same time—one that requires you to play many games simultaneously *and* play many in quick succession. The current Internet is such a battleground. Imagine too that the pace never slows, it only grows faster and faster. The Internet is growing and changing exponentially. Your competitors can change during the game—they can become bigger, stronger, smarter, and faster. New competitors can emerge from thin air to enter the game against you. You can coax them into joining your side, but they can simultaneously play both for and against you. As if this game isn't difficult enough, there are still more challenges. The many concurrent games can mutate while they are in progress—a game may start as one you know and recognize, but finish in an entirely different form.

Your firm's dynamic competitive business environment is much like this game. *This is why you must strategically place your firm at the best juncture created by all the competitive variables*—including converging industries, new technologies, merging competitors, and ever-changing national and global protectionism. The tangled intricacies of multination, multifirm, and multiindustry convergence dictate a multidimensional position to best maximize revenue and profit gains. You can't stand still and simply hide in your niche business. You must continually reevaluate the competitive landscape and be adaptable enough to quickly reposition your firm in the ebb and flow of ever-changing opportunities and threats.

Let's explore the benefits of a multistrategy approach by reviewing how much the now-outdated strategic traditional "wisdom" continues to rule or blindside many companies. Traditional strategy models have long claimed that firms must forge a strategy at either end of a one-dimensional spectrum—low cost at one end of the spectrum and differentiation at the opposite end—but never aim at hitting both ends simultaneously. These old models forced companies into two distinct camps—a company could either focus on becoming the low-cost provider of its goods or services, or it could provide consumers many choices through a customization or differentiation strategy. The strategic battle cry became, "You can't be stuck in the middle. You will fail there." While this traditional view may have served a noble purpose for past generations, all too often it will *doom* companies that embrace it now. Today's most successful firms continuously match the complexity of their strategies to the complexity of their competitive landscape.

Consider the highly successful dual strategy combination of both low-cost and customization now available in just one product line at The Home Depot, Inc. In its kitchen design center, customers are offered up an endless array of kitchen configurations through three-dimensional design software. As two newlyweds look at a large computer screen and describe their dream kitchen, a Home Depot service representative navigates through the easy-to-use kitchen design program, moving cabinetry and appliances into any arrangement the couple can imagine. The shoppers can ultimately end up with a kitchen design that is unique and customized for just them. And then, all components of the kitchen can be ordered, delivered, and installed by Home Depot, the industry low-cost leader.

Just one generation ago, these same kitchen shoppers would have had to call on the unique talents of an architect or general contractor for such a design. But through today's advanced software technology and the panoramic perspective at Home Depot, both low cost and custom design can be accomplished by the very same firm.

Much like Home Depot, British Airways' (BA) dual-pronged strategy targets simultaneously both the high-profit first-class traveler and—via discount airline GO Fly Ltd. (GO)—the low-budget traveler, forging BA's participation in two normally separate markets. By capturing both extremes of the demand curve BA forces other players to fight with each other while being "stuck in the middle." Other budget start-up airlines in Britain have loudly complained that BA's GO subsidiary is pricing seats below cost in a classic predatory pricing maneuver to drive them out of business. But in fact, because BA already has a huge infrastructure of airline equipment, gates, routes, bulk suppliers of everything it needs, and an advanced computer reservation system, there are only marginal extra costs it needs to invest in GO to make it a brilliant success. In fact, BA's blended cost is no doubt lower because GO uses nonunion crews and used planes. And so BA, via this dual pronged strategy, achieves a higher total blended profit than its first class rivals, low budget competitors, or average airlines stuck with only a middle-ground strategy.

Many other firms have adopted a similar dual-pronged strategy, for it captures both extremes of the demand curve and forces competitors to be left fighting for the crowded middle ground. For example, DaimlerChrysler deliberately set its sights on these same distinct customer markets—to be both low-cost producer via Chrysler and retain its luxury Mercedes image while simultaneously reaping continually lower total blended costs from its combined operations and higher total profits from its blended depth and wide range of product offerings.

Today, many of the most advanced corporations, such as Intel, have adopted composite strategies targeted to their specific, but distinct, lines of business to beat competitors in much the same manner as Home Depot and British Airways. It is no longer simply an "either-or" world where firms focus only on low cost versus differentiation or just one end of the economics demand curve. To embrace such a narrow view today in complex and brutally competitive global markets would be like fighting with one hand tied behind your back. For example, mass-consumer bicycles, cars, clothes, tools, and cameras are now produced in the most high-tech factories on the very same computerized manufacturing equipment that makes personally customized versions of the same product for elite individual buyers who are willing to pay three to five times the price of the mass market version. Electronically controlled commands can insert a variety of highly customized bikes, suits, or cars into a long production run of a high-volume version. By being able to manufacture both mass-market and "elite" products on the same advanced equipment with a change-over of only fractions of a second between types of goods, the firm is able not only to earn a significantly higher blended profit margin and total profit, but can also reduce overall costs because most production supplies and components are ordered in bulk quantities. In short, these state-of-the-art technologies make possible successful composite strategies because the same computerized machine that lowers the overall cost of goods produced also improves the total quality and customized orders, and increases the total rate of return of the corporation.

At Toyota Motor Corp.'s Georgetown, Kentucky, assembly plant they recognized the competitive advantage of being able to match production schedules with individual customer purchases. In the past, Toyota's paint shops had produced a "batch" of each color car. They made white cars, then red, then green, and so on, regardless of customer buying patterns. With the estimated volume for each color scheduled weeks in advance, they often found that production schedules had to be rearranged because some colors sold more, and some less than the forecasted volume. In order to hedge against the inaccuracy of the forecasts, a large "safety stock" of each color car was held in inventory, which tied up tens of millions of dollars. When Toyota built its new plant in Georgetown the paint shop was constructed with state-of-the-art, quick-change equipment that allowed the production schedules to more closely match actual car buyers' purchase orders. This sophisticated system was so flexible it could paint just one car, wash out the paint lines and spray guns, paint another car a different color, wash out again, paint yet another color, and so on. The new system could be changed from one color to the next in just *three seconds*. More important, it could paint a red car, wash out, and then paint a white car. Toyota's production quality standards were vital, because if even minute traces of red paint contaminated the white, the result would be Toyota's first pink-streaked cars.

Toyota's state-of-the-art paint system was initially quite expensive. Don't assume, however, that huge capital expenditures are a necessity for creating both mass production efficiencies and small lot production. Consider another business where color is even more important—in the cosmetics industry. At Procter & Gamble's Hunt Valley, Maryland, cosmetics manufacturing facility, rapid change-over was achieved not with money, but with the expertise and creativity of dedicated technicians. In its nail polish filling and packaging business, P&G was confronted with a "selection versus inventory" dilemma similar to Toyota's.

Because color cosmetics follow the fast-changing fashion world, inventories of specific cosmetic shades can quickly become slow-moving or even obsolete. Finished goods of shades that are either out of season or are no longer fashionable take up valuable warehouse space and restrict cash flows. P&G needed to keep just the right amount of over 125 different shades of nail polish in stock—enough to meet short-term demand, but not *too* much. Quick change-over between shades and small lot production while simultaneously meeting customers' ever-changing demands became a necessity.

After basic training in quick-change methods and short-cycle manufacturing processes, a team of motivated technicians created innovative procedures to severely cut change-over time. The technicians combined their many years of experience operating and maintaining the nail polish production line equipment with their new knowledge about quick change-over methods to totally redesign production schedules and procedures. Their results were fantastic—change-over time was reduced by 70 percent while absolutely *no* money was spent on new equipment. By reducing change-over time, the team was able to drastically reduce lot size for production runs of each shade while maintaining large order production efficiencies.

At first glance, the results at both Toyota and P&G may not appear to be that amazing. But just consider a critical characteristic of the primary material used in each operation—both nail polish and automotive paint are *extremely* flammable. So flammable, in fact, that they must be confined to equipment and locations that have been specifically built to meet "explosion proof" manufacturing and building codes. Each piece of equipment, including every electric motor, contact, or switch, is engineered so that no electric spark can come in contact with the highly explosive paint fumes. Telephones in these areas must also meet stringent and exacting codes, and even all hand tools are made of bronze, a metal that will not create a spark when it is hit against another metal. These quick-change projects still had to meet every safety standard and account for each change, no matter how minor, in these operations that are commonly referred to as "hazardous systems."

P&G added still another facet to this portion of its composite strategy. The change-over project in the nail polish operation owed much of its success to powerful internal benchmarking. Liquid makeup filling and packaging, a sister operation located in the very same facility, had started a quick change-over project about ten months earlier, and the nail polish business reapplied its knowledge and techniques.

Again, through skill and motivation, another group of talented technicians had solved the liquid makeup change-over challenge by designing and building an ingenious "crash cart" to drastically cut change-over time. This mobile makeup delivery system could be easily rolled in and out of the manufacturing line. The team built an exact duplicate of the cart so one could be cleaned while the other was used in the filling operation. Within a few short months, change-over time was slashed from two and a half hours to just eighteen minutes, and ultimately to an extraordinary four minutes. This allowed the team to deliver a greater selection of makeup shades in a much more compressed time frame. Incredibly, the "crash carts" cost the team just $5,000. The key to the success of this flexibility project at P&G was the talent and motivation of empowered technicians. While four minutes certainly cannot compare to the three seconds that Toyota achieved, just consider the impact on both inventory reductions and flexibility by reducing change-over time by more than 97 percent—all for $5,000. The technicians then doubled the benefit by passing their experience and knowledge on to co-workers.

All these firms—Home Depot, British Airways, Toyota, P&G, as well as Dell Computer with its build-to-order, not build-to-inventory business model—have achieved market leadership by casting aside the tightly held tradition that firms could be either low cost producers or customized small lot producers, but never both. They all embraced a panoramic perspective that boldly proclaimed, "We can be both. We must continuously remain capable of being both. Because by doing so, we will devastate our competition!"

The composite strategy needed to win in the consolidating world challenges deeply imbedded traditional wisdom in just the same manner these examples challenged low cost versus customization. The "eat or be eaten" wisdom presents an "either-or" view of the consolidating landscape. Nothing could be more restrictive to your firm's range of strategic alternatives. You must be ready, willing, and able to strike using the full magnitude of strategies to both exploit merging competitors and execute your own mergers and merger alternatives with excellence.

Your composite strategy must aim at several targets simultaneously. Just like the "smart" bombs used to attack highly precise targets in the air war of Desert Storm, different strategies and tools must be deployed to hit your multiple targets. Consider the warfare of World War II—the same types of weapons were used for a wide variety of purposes, and these weapons were reasonably effective for some uses but nearly totally ineffective for most others. The technology introduced in Desert Storm, however, demonstrated the surgical precision of smart bombs: They were used to attack very specific strategic targets, they rarely missed, and they created minimal collateral damage.

One important characteristic of those firms that implement the most successful composite strategies is their progressive approach to leadership—they *all* push leadership responsibilities far deeper into their organizations than do "traditional" firms. Any company that isolates leadership to just a handful of top executives will find the composite strategy far more difficult, *even impossible,* to implement. When you provide the skills, expectations, and accountability for leading critical strategic components to people deeper within your organization, you build the capability to implement more strategies simultaneously.

Imagine a long, several-day drive across a parched, sun-baked desert. This particular drive, however, has a challenging twist—gas stations are not placed where you would expect or need them. In fact, they can suddenly appear for just a few moments and then quickly vanish, and there is absolutely no map or other indication to show when and where they will appear. If you pass an opportunity to re-fuel, or just to "top off" your gas tank, you have no way of knowing when the next fueling opportunity will present itself. If you forego a chance for fuel, you run a risk of running out of gas and not being able to finish the drive.

Strategic opportunities in the consolidating world are much like these "here one minute, gone the next" gas stations on your desert journey. The windows of opportunity for strategic attacks are small and close quickly. More importantly, if you do not exploit an opportunity, your direct competitors *will* exploit it. This gives *them* additional "fuel" that could have been *yours.* There are no neutral choices here. You must leverage the best opportunities to gain competitive advantage, otherwise you risk handing the double-edged sword to your competitors. Your ability to expand your firm's capacity to both identify and exploit opportunities is crucial to your strategic flexibility and responsiveness.

General Electric has completed over six hundred acquisitions during Jack Welch's rein. This could only be accomplished because Welch drove authority and strategic empowerment well down into his organization. With many eyes searching for strategic opportunities, all branches of the many businesses inside the entire GE company have the ability to quickly identify and act upon countless acquisition targets and many other opportunities throughout the world. No firm that limits its strategic leadership to strategic planners or top executives could ever seize opportunities as GE has done. In the coming years you will be able to see the long-lasting power of GE as it rides the wave of economic and financial recovery out of Japan and all of Asia that has resulted from the almost $20 billion it invested in its many acquisitions, joint ventures, and alliances during the Asian economic crisis.

MICHAEL ARMSTRONG'S BATTLEGROUND

Complex firms in complex industries will not survive without a composite strategy. No long-established sector has seen more rapid change and become more complex than the telecommunications industry. Giant leaps in technology, new strategic and technological links to many other industries, changes in communication delivery channels, and diverging and converging networks of firms have created a competitive landscape fraught with both minefields and opportunities. No telecom CEO ever embarked upon a more complex composite strategy than Michael Armstrong at AT&T. After joining the company in November 1997, Armstrong swiftly crafted a sweeping, comprehensive, and intricate strategy. Within a few short months he was simultaneously doing acquisitions, divestitures, joint ventures, alliances, franchise agreements, driving breakthrough internal change, as well as exploiting merger failures of others. (See Appendix H for details of Armstrong's first eighteen months at AT&T.)

Armstrong's composite corporate strategy for AT&T took the same skill, attention to detail, surgical precision, and understanding of interrelationships that the diamond cutter uses to create the most brilliant precious gem from a lifeless rock. The telecommunications industry was being reinvented before his very eyes and Armstrong knew a static or one-dimensional strategy would spell financial ruin for AT&T. He had to move fast and aggressively on several fronts simultaneously. *He knew he could not wait.*

As discussed in Chapter 4, Armstrong used the WorldCom/MCI merger as the external threat for driving AT&T's rapid and far-reaching internal changes. Armstrong saw that no single strategy would allow AT&T to fully leverage the rich opportunities created by waves of changing technologies, consolidating markets, and array of new interdependencies in cable television, communications satellites, Internet portals, plus local, long-distance, and wireless communications. AT&T owned 60 percent of the long-distance market, but with an army of new competitors and shrinking margins, Armstrong knew that continued dependence on just long-distance didn't have the horsepower needed to generate more than low, single digit growth. In a series of bold, decisive moves, he struck quickly to create opportunities in the local and wireless telephone, cable television, and Internet markets. Within the same week, Armstrong forged marketing alliances with some of the Internet's most active portals—Infoseek Corp., Lycos Inc., and Excite Inc. Two weeks later he signed a marketing partnership with Yahoo! Inc. to further expand AT&T's presence with Internet users. In just three weeks, AT&T's name and services were served up to the nearly 78 million visitors to Yahoo!, Infoseek, Lycos, and Excite per month.[1]

Armstrong made the boldest moves of any long-distance phone company into the very markets the 1996 Telecommunications Act was originally designed to jump start. In the complicated telecom infrastructure, the elusive "last mile" of wire into homes was exclusively owned by the Baby Bells, GTE, and other local phone companies. They proved to be tough negotiators, demanding substantial payments for access rights to their lines. AT&T was paying 40 cents of every long-distance revenue dollar in access fees alone.[2] Armstrong knew he had to find a better alternative.

Through three major acquisition announcements in 1998 and 1999, Armstrong guided AT&T on a daring "end run" that stunned the Baby Bells and the entire telecommunications industry. First, AT&T purchased Teleport Communications Group for $11.3 billion. Teleport made AT&T an immediate local phone service provider in the nation's sixty largest urban centers, including corporate business gems New York City and Los Angeles. Even bolder was AT&T's purchase of the nation's second largest cable television carrier, Tele-Communications, Inc. (TCI). For $37.3 billion, AT&T completely sidestepped the Baby Bells' coveted "last mile" of telephone wire into homes and businesses. Through TCI, AT&T now had broad-band cable connections into 22 million subscribing homes and TCI's stake in the prized At Home Corp., a high-speed "always connected" cable Internet service with exclusive contracts with many U.S. cable TV firms. As a third step of AT&T's last-mile effort, Armstrong spent $58 billion to acquire cable giant MediaOne. This gave AT&T the perfect digital platform for selling a bundle of communications services including long-distance and local phone service, Internet access, on-line banking, and cable television. In three swift moves, Armstrong gained first mover advantage over other long-distance carriers and was poised to quickly crack the $100 billion local phone business. But acquisitions were not the final component of Armstrong's daring composite strategy. AT&T was also aggressively marketing its services through franchising agreements with numerous local and wireless phone companies.

Armstrong also divested certain businesses. He sold AT&T's paging unit to MetroCall and its stake in DirecTV Inc. back to Hughes Electronics. Of greater impact was the sale of AT&T's underperforming Universal Card credit card business unit to Citicorp for an astonishing $4 billion—twice what analysts had predicted it would fetch.[3] Armstrong orchestrated an incredibly smooth deal by leveraging the attractiveness of AT&T's strong brand recognition: he got Citicorp to agree to pay almost $1 billion over ten years for a licensing agreement to keep AT&T's name on the card. They also agreed to continue the two-cards-in-one combination credit/calling card AT&T had pioneered. The deal had one final highly valuable component—AT&T and Citicorp would work together to offer on-line banking via the Internet in the future.[4]

Armstrong continued his broad sweeping agenda. Using aggressive lobbying skills gained as chairman of Hughes Corp., he simultaneously played both offense and defense—he attacked by urging federal regulators to reject the announced Baby Bell mergers of Bell Atlantic Corp. and GTE Corp. and also SBC Communications and Ameritech Corp. Armstrong also argued with the same regulators *not* to allow America Online and others open access to the broadband cable communication wires he was so ferociously protecting. Armstrong then announced a worldwide alliance with British Telecommunications PLC that would produce an estimated $11 billion in revenue in its first year of operation—with only $1 billion of capital investment. Finally, Armstrong closed out his first year at AT&T with the acquisition of International Business Machines Corp.'s global networking system for $5 billion to secure many of the world's blue chip corporations as customers for AT&T's Internet services as well as its total range of other communications services.

Armstrong's composite strategy was bold, lightning quick, and difficult to implement. It was a highly detailed network of interrelated strategies to place AT&T at the best possible crossroads in the convergence of telecommunication, cable television, and the Internet. By early 1999, just over fifteen months after Armstrong was hired, AT&T's market capitalization had risen over 100 percent to $168 billion, an all time high.[5] As the new year dawned, the pace of his deal-making frenzy never slowed—with joint venture agreements with five regional cable companies and a planned deal with Comcast on the table, AT&T will secure access to a grand total of over 25 million cable customers in the United States.[6] Armstrong's strategy to offer a bundle of communications services through broad-band cable lines was fast becoming a reality. His next top priority was to drastically improve cable television set-top boxes in order to offer telephone and Internet broad-band, high-speed capability at a tiny fraction of today's cost. Once again, Armstrong was forging a cluster of strategic alliances and acquisitions to attack his goal.

But AT&T was facing many formidable foes, most notably MCI WorldCom. The war between Armstrong and MCI WorldCom's CEO Bernie Ebbers was like an attack-counterattack battle. In 1999 MCI WorldCom announced its $129 billion purchase of Sprint, giving Ebbers a fast-growing wireless business needed to complete his stable of telecommunications services. While Armstrong placed his

AT&T vs. MCI WorldCom

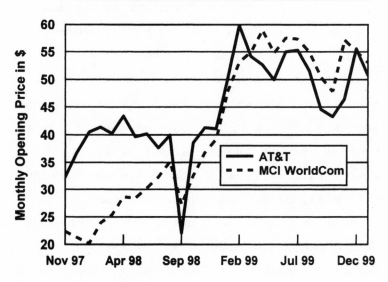

Source: Yahoo!Finance

Note: Monthly opening prices adjusted for dividends and splits

bet on cable, Ebbers clearly believed wireless would be the chosen telecommunication delivery method in the future. Only time will tell which strategy will prove to be the bigger winner.

The stakes are high and only one firm can be number one in a telecommunications industry that is being continuously reinvented. The Vodaphone/Mannesmann merger increased the complexity on this battlefield tenfold. With this merger, Vodaphone captured the lead in the worldwide cellular phone market with 42 million customers in Europe and the U.S. The blockbuster $183 billion merger of America Online and Time Warner added yet another dimension to the battle. AOL's Steve Case didn't want his Internet service to be blocked from broadband access. The Time Warner acquisition immediately vaulted

AOL into the number two cable provider position behind AT&T. Fear drove him to make, at the time, the world's largest acquisition.

Steve Case commandingly positioned his firm where neither AT&T nor MCI WorldCom could compete head-to-head with AOL/Time Warner. Not only did Case now guarantee communications *access* to customers, he could also provide the *content* made available from Time Warner, the world's largest media company. AOL subscribers would now have access to all the news, books, movies and magazines in Time Warner's huge portfolio. In one quick move, Case had positioned AOL at the critical intersection of the Internet and media industries—a critical juncture where neither AT&T nor MCI WorldCom could fully compete. Vodaphone is currently orchestrating a complicated strategic alliance network—primarily with Vivendi of France—so they too will be able to provide content along with telecom and Internet access.

JACK WELCH'S GENERAL ELECTRIC—SEIZING OPPORTUNITY AT EVERY TURN

Much of General Electric's total strength is derived from its ability to identify and implement multiple initiatives simultaneously. GE weaves together marketing and strategic strengths with the ability to execute with extraordinary operational excellence. The result is a dynamic flexibility and powerful competitive advantages to the firm. Jack Welch has coined the term "smart bombing" to describe GE's worldwide composite strategy. GE creates a hybrid mix of strategies, products, and marketing to best take advantage of the revenue and profit opportunities in each market.[7]

Jack Welch's GE: 1981-2000

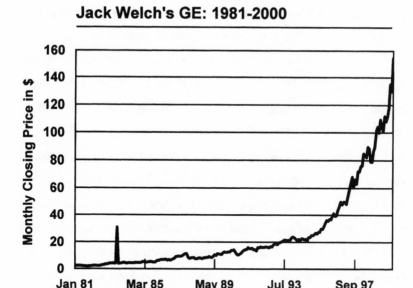

Source: Yahoo!Finance
Note: Monthly closing prices adjusted for dividends and splits

Under Welch, GE delivered the results of a fast-growth company, increasing its market value from $12 billion in 1981 to over $500 billion by the end of 1999.[8] *Fortune* magazine reported that not even Intel's Intel's Andrew S. Grove, nor Walt Disney's Michael D. Eisner nor Berkshire Hathaway's Warren E. Buffett, nor even the late Coca-Cola chieftain Roberto C. Goizueta nor the late Wal-Mart founder Sam Walton had created more shareholder value than Jack Welch."[9] What makes Welch's accomplishment even more stunning is that many of GE's businesses are in long-established, entrenched, and mature markets like power generation, household appliances, jet engines, locomotives, and light bulbs. In fact, GE is the only remaining firm of the original twelve that that comprised the first Dow Jones Industrial Average in 1896.

One significant key to GE's success is its ability to identify opportunities and then control virtually every component in each of its specifically chosen business markets. In the Aircraft Engine unit, for example, GE starts by making one of the most reliable and efficient engines with diagnostic technologies surpassing those of Pratt & Whitney (United Technologies Corp.) and Rolls-Royce PLC. But GE does not rest on its engineering and manufacturing mastery alone. Through GE Capital Services, they can provide either large order jet engine or jet fleet financing or leasing at below market rates. Additionally, because of the "boundaryless" organization design fostered by Welch, the financial unit isn't just a group of lending experts—many also have extensive experience in the inner workings of the jet engine industry as well. Through the in-flight remote engine diagnostic capability, GE's service technicians can monitor every jet engine's actual performance in the air or on the ground, anywhere on the globe. This is a secret weapon in GE's airline service contract business, which will help drive down the airlines' total maintenance costs. To further expand their reach, GE offers the same service expertise to any jet engine made by one of its competitors. Not only can the airlines then deal with just one engine service provider, but GE gets to learn every minute detail about the engines manufactured by the competition.

GE continually mines the globe for extraordinary opportunities in every business. They make many small acquisitions in order to provide one-stop shopping for all customers, ranging from major corporations to individuals. For instance, GE home mortgage lenders can make multiple sales to new homeowners in a way that makes life easy for the customer and much more profitable for GE. Imagine a telephone call from just one GE salesperson: "Thank you for choosing GE to finance the mortgage on your new home. Would you like mortgage insurance to protect your family in case you unexpectedly pass away? Would you also like to insure your home and its contents through GE? How about life insurance or insurance for your car? And we can supply your home with top-rated GE kitchen and laundry appliances at a discount, and then provide peace of mind through our expert service contracts. We can bundle all your needs together, reduce your total expenses, and you can write just one check for all these products and services each month." Knowing GE, it will not be long before remote diagnostics for its appliances will prompt a service call even before a GE appliance has a chance to malfunction.

GE captures far more profit-making opportunities than its competition. Through "value migration," every GE unit expands the very definition of its market and then creates a vast array of new high-margin services. By offering maintenance service, long term (10–12 year) service contracts, management consulting, and even category management, customers become ever dependent on their partnership with GE. Not only does GE create additional profits, it helps its business customers boost their own profitability.

At Home Depot, GE created the first nation-wide major appliance home delivery channel that linked GE factories directly to the final consumer. Through this new process, Home Depot's appliance sales grew 25–50 percent in every store, GE's share per store jumped to 70 percent, delivery costs dropped by 60 percent, and customer satisfaction soared to more than 90 percent. By expanding the definition of its appliance business, GE discovered new opportunities to please both Home Depot and consumers while earning additional revenue and profit. GE continually reinvents its equation for market dominance.

Another facet of GE's composite strategy is that it is in a perpetual state of strike readiness. In 1998 GE Capital announced a plan to seize many opportunities from the rubble of financial and business disasters. As the Asian financial crisis was spreading its impact throughout the globe, GE Capital saw bargain basement prices 75 percent below the recent market, and started a scavenger hunt for a series of Asian finance and leasing company acquisitions. As the world's largest non-bank lender, GE Capital planned to use the Asian crisis to grow GE Capital Asia Pacific Ltd. from $4 billion to a projected $20 billion in assets by 2003.[10]

When we look at GE's masterful approach to its comprehensive, complex, and dynamic strategies to control all facets of its individual businesses, it becomes clear that no profit making or customer service stone is left unturned. GE's medical unit just introduced a new, highly sophisticated computer tomography (CT) scanner that reduces full body scanning to just 20 seconds. It costs 50 percent more than any other scanner, but with its incredible speed, busy hospitals will find the total ROI quite appealing. At the same time, GE also introduced the world's very *least expensive* CT scanner. At just $200,000 it is priced within the buying power of many less-well-financed medical facilities throughout the world. Costing more than 50 percent less than the nearest competitor's, this economical scanner opens a whole new market. With the introduction of these two CT scanners, GE hits two separate targets simultaneously. In essence, GE controls the most basic forces described by Michael Porter in his famous Five Forces model—the bargaining power of suppliers, the bargaining power of buyers, rivalry with industry competitors, threat of substitutes or the threat of new entrants. Through an integrated weaving of comprehensive strategies and near-flawless quality execution, GE stands ready to take on all challengers. But potential competitors had best develop an incredible plan—not only has GE been named *Fortune* magazine's Most Admired Company; in 1998 a *Financial Times* survey named GE the most respected company in the entire world. In fact, it earned twice as many votes as the second place firm.[11]

Michael Armstrong and Jack Welch are not the only CEOs using complicated composite strategies—so are many others in pharmaceuticals, aerospace, defense, media, cable, telecommunications, automotive, and financial services. Both GM and Ford have announced plans to match Toyota's five-day build-to-order initiative. Toyota is launching an on-line brokerage service aimed to build even more recognition of the famous Toyota name.

In an unprecedented move, GM, Ford, and DaimlerChrysler announced an industry-wide Internet business-to-business (B2B) venture to radically reduce purchasing costs. With combined annual purchases of $240 billion, this joint venture created the world's largest Internet company. The venture will only continue to grow, as it is open to other car makers and all automotive parts suppliers. If fully utilized by all auto industry companies, this venture will easily surpass $740 billion in annual purchases. This Internet-based B2B procurement exchange model is exploding in all industries, including pharmaceuticals, aerospace, healthcare, medical devices, chemicals, steel, paper, and retail.

For giant firms, a composite strategy is virtually required in today's complex, fast changing, segmented global business environment. Brutal competition and relentless pressure to achieve speed to market have forced many firms to convert rapidly to composite strategies. But small and medium-size firms are not excluded from doing business in a complex environment. Composite strategy is a tool for navigating in a complex world, *regardless of size.* The Internet alone is creating competitive threats for many businesses that just a few years ago could find all their market competitors listed in the local telephone directory.

If you execute these composite strategies adroitly by carefully targeting each separate strategy to different products in different industries, sectors, or foreign nations, you can provide dynamic flexibility and powerful competitive advantages to your firm. Used effectively, the composite strategy can maximize a firm's revenues and profits derived from all its different businesses throughout the globe. Yet this combination of key strategies is extremely complex and difficult to implement. Managers must acquire the prerequisite knowledge and skill in each of the five previously described strategies before they can effectively design a composite strategy.

Your firm's composite strategy must meet the several unique challenges of a continually reinvented global business arena. Your firm must be very focused on hitting two or more specific moving targets. And your composite strategy must not only be planned in advance, but will require regular updating under dynamic surveillance.

8

The Future Consolidating World

Your personal risk in the consolidating world is growing larger and more dangerous with each passing day. Worldwide rampant consolidation is gathering steam and will continue to propel itself forward at record rates. Your success as a manager hinges upon your ability to navigate, lead, and deliver business results in a world where no one can hide from the impact of consolidation and its continuous transformation of the competitive landscape.

Even well respected managers with sterling track records of business success have fallen victim when they suddenly found their strategic and operational skills lacking the array of new essential tools needed to help them win in today's consolidating world. Bayerische Motoren Werke AG (BMW) chairman Bernd Pischetsrieder learned just how easily a botched acquisition could bring his once successful career crashing to a halt. Pischetsrieder had been widely hailed as a strategic genius because he made BMW into the first international car company to offer vehicles in *every* market niche, a strategic move that all other car makers jumped to follow. But his leadership of BMW's financially struggling Rover unit in the U.K. proved to be his downfall. Purchased in 1994, Rover added mass market sedans, prestigious luxury sport utility vehicles (SUVs), tiny city cars, and even the MG two-seat sports car to BMW's existing stable of luxury sedans. But the acquisition was a struggle from the very start. Even the popular Range Rover and Land Rover, so desirable in the white-hot U.S. SUV market, couldn't push Rover into profitability. Rover assembly factories had been plagued with constant poor quality and inefficiencies. BMW's ownership did nothing to reverse these troubling manufacturing problems. They failed to cross-pollinate the efficiencies found in BMW's German and U.S. factories. By 1998, the losses at Rover resulted in BMW's first decline in net profit since 1993. BMW cars were enjoying record sales, but overall corporate profits were sagging. In early 1999, when rumors first surfaced that Pischetsrieder would be fired, BMW stock shot up 6.5 percent. Just a few days later, the rumors proved true and his career at BMW was finished, all the result of a failed acquisition. Then in the Spring of 2000, BMW finally pulled the plug on Rover, selling it to Ford and venture capitalists Alchemy Partners while being forced to write-off over $3 billion. Rover, which BMW insiders had nicknamed "The English Patient," was a complete and total acquisition failure.

Many other managers with a long, successful tenure found themselves on equally thin ice. Ron Woodward, president of Boeing's Commercial Airplane Group during the disastrous acquisition of McDonnell Douglas, was given his pink slip after thirty years of laudable service. Boards of directors have very little tolerance for botched consolidation—the impact on revenue, profit, and shareholder wealth is far too significant for them to ignore. Furthermore, CEOs are not the only people who receive extra-intense performance evaluations during mismanaged merger integration. Jamie Dimon, longtime second-in-command to Sandy Weill, took the fall when the Travelers/Citicorp marriage stumbled during its first months. Larry Clarkson at Boeing had just been appointed president of Boeing Enterprises (airline maintenance services) when he followed his boss, Ron Woodward, into early retirement. At BMW, Bernd Pischetsrieder's heir apparent Wolfgang Reitzle also received his walking papers, as did Rover's head Walter Hasselkus.

Managers at every level can see their careers derailed by poorly managed consolidation. However, we don't see the very real and painful cascade of hundreds or thousands of damaged careers throughout an organization during or following a disastrous merger integration because the press only focuses their spotlight on the very top executives. Much like the spillover effect to assistant coaches and players when a head coach is fired in professional sports, a chain reaction of widespread career damage is a common result.

The danger of merger failure is not exclusively reserved for just those firms that drive blind into the challenge of merger integration. Even when firms try to use fast-track type principles and tools to orchestrate a successful integration, there is still a real potential the road will be full of with potholes. Computer Associates (CA) developed a proven acquisition process that helped them post an average annual return that surpassed Microsoft, Coca-Cola, and Gillette. CA had a long history of successful acquisitions—until they attempted to purchase Computer Sciences, Inc. in 1998. CA's past acquisition targets had been companies that were normally in disarray and unlikely to remain viable without CA. Computer Sciences, however, was different. It was much larger than CA's past targets, it was extremely healthy, and it knew just how to throw a textbook defense against a hostile suitor. Within less than a month of its attempted hostile takeover, CA folded its cards and backed away. Wall Street quickly stripped CA of its "Great Acquirer" title, and by the end of the year CA's shareholder return fell a disappointing 19.4 percent.[1]

We have also trumpeted the expert crafting of strategies and operational plans at both DaimlerChrysler and AT&T. Yet, they too are having significant problems along their journey as key executives have left to join direct competitors. Before Michael Armstrong became CEO, AT&T had stumbled for years through a string of problem acquisitions, including a total failure with NCR Corp. and the McCaw Cellular debacle when the McCaw management team quickly departed en masse. Yet even with hard-driving, aggressive Armstrong at the helm, Robert Annunziata, president of AT&T's business services group, suddenly quit in early 1999 to become CEO of two-year-old Global Crossing Ltd. His departure was a stunning loss for Armstrong's top executive team. At the same time, *The Wall Street Journal* broke a front page story that chronicled the ongoing management style clashes between John Zeglis, AT&T's president and Leo Hindery, head of AT&T's cable business. Zeglis, a buttoned-down AT&T veteran, is a virtual polar opposite of the back-slapping, "our handshake is our contract" Hindery. The loss of either man could be a devastating blow to Armstrong's aggressive plans. In fact, Hindery, the most respected cable industry veteran, did leave to become chairman and CEO of Global Crossing's

140

Internet arm GlobalCenter, Inc. Annunziata knew the power of the magnet strategy as he worked to build a direct competition to AT&T.

At DaimlerChrysler, three top executives, including vice presidents of platform engineering, international/mini-van manufacturing, and corporate communications, jumped ship and ran off to join General Motors or Ford. By the fall of 1999, DaimlerChrysler's integration was dealt an even more severe blow—in a shake-up of the company's supervisory board, four of seventeen members were released, including Thomas Stallkamp, president of the company's North American unit. Stallkamp's departure was widely seen as a huge setback to the integration and to morale throughout the company. He had been rumored to be chairman Juergen Shrempp's heir apparent and a was key leader in the integration. But Stallkamp publicly criticized Shrempp's decisions, including the deliberately quick pace of the merger integration. Additionally, Stallkamp and Shrempp failed to reconcile their conflicting decision-making approaches. So hard-charging Schrempp decided it was time to streamline the supervisory board—without Stallkamp. DaimlerChrysler's long-term challenge then became stopping a mass exodus of other top U.S. managers.

In light of DaimlerChrysler's publicly announced intent to become the world's largest car company by 2003, it must stop additional losses of talented employees. Additionally, becoming number one will undoubtedly hinge upon rapid expansion into Asia, which is expected to produce 70 percent of the global auto market growth until 2005. With both Honda's and Toyota's aversion to mergers, DaimlerChrysler will probably use an array of strategies if it is to have a chance of meeting its aggressive goal. Juergen Schrempp's original global strategy that included his high-tech merger war room—built to connect Daimler to strategic sites throughout the world—will allow DaimlerChrysler to enter into multiple strategic alliances, joint ventures and additional acquisitions. In early 2000, DaimlerChrysler entered into a bidding contest against GM, Ford, Hyundai, and Fiat to buy Daewoo, the debt-ridden South Korean car manufacturer. Daewoo's high-tech factories are currently among the most advanced and cost efficient in the world. Additionally, two of its manufacturing plants are ideally located in Poland and Korea. DaimlerChrysler finally established the critical Asian foothold when it purchased controlling interest in Mitsubishi Motors.

But what kind of manager is the one who will succeed in the face of such a seemingly endless series of merger Mt. Everests? It is no longer true to say that only the strong leaders can survive. Instead, survival is accomplished through highly flexible, very current, and fast teams who are extremely knowledgeable about the powerful forces that are driving industry consolidation and have a deep understanding of merger failure history. Not only must you embrace the dynamic panoramic perspective and have an arsenal of strategic and operational tools at your disposal, but you and your team must be prepared for the rapid-fire series of competitive challenges that will result from the emerging global consolidation revolution. Global combination is now in its *infancy.* You can expect to see worldwide roll-ups with speed and intensity not unlike many national roll-ups of highly fragmented local businesses. The world's thousands of businesses are still extremely fragmented. The forces of consolidation now have two critical components required to ignite the race across the globe like a wildfire: the support of highly advanced commerce and communications tech-

Long-standing U.S. Oligopolies

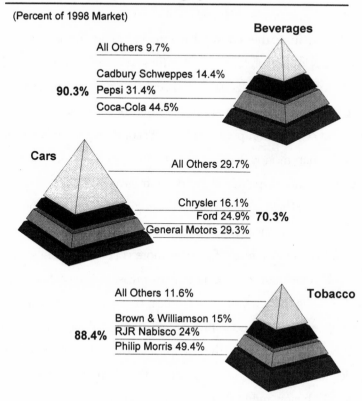

(Percent of 1998 Market)

Beverages

All Others 9.7%

Cadbury Schweppes 14.4%

90.3% Pepsi 31.4%

Coca-Cola 44.5%

Cars

All Others 29.7%

Chrysler 16.1%

Ford 24.9% **70.3%**

General Motors 29.3%

All Others 11.6% **Tobacco**

Brown & Williamson 15%

88.4% RJR Nabisco 24%

Philip Morris 49.4%

Data Source: G. Pascal Zachary, "Let's Play Oligopoly," *The Wall Street Journal,* March 8, 1999, p. B1.

nology and the simultaneous crashing of many long-standing social and political walls of national protectionism.

Past waves of mergers and acquisitions have resulted in many industries settling into a comfortable handful of major players. In the United States, oligopolies have been the desired competitive arrangement of CEOs for generations. In automotive manufacturing, there's the Big Three. Accounting has its Big Five. Ninety percent of the soft drink industry is owned by just three players. Six movie studios have controlled 90 percent of the film industry for sixty years. Five companies produce almost all of the world's recorded music. As industries mature, they consolidate into a few giant firms.

Business leaders prefer oligopolies for several reasons. First, a small number of competitors is easier to keep an eye upon. The chance of being blindsided by a new product, service, or technology is reduced when the competition pool is smaller. Second, oligopoly is *far* more desirable than monopoly because governments don't feel compelled to force the same type of regulatory controls as they do upon single-firm markets. There is substantially less regulation and far more freedom. And finally, having competition keeps a CEO's organization on its toes. Competitive forces foster far more cost consciousness, innovation, and speed of execution than any pressure from a chief executive. With oligopoly, a CEO has the best of all worlds—few (but just enough) competitors and minimal regulation. Even the 1984 breakup of Ma Bell didn't withstand the oligopoly inertia—the 1998 SBC Communications/Ameritech and GTE/Bell Atlantic mergers, both valued at over $70 billion, reduced the Baby Bells by two.

The entire world is now marching toward *global* oligopolies. The mega-mergers of Mobil/Exxon, British Petroleum/Amoco, Vodaphone/AirTouch Communications/Mannesmann and Daimler-Benz/Chrysler foreshadow what you can expect to see in the next decade. Johns Hopkins University business historian Louis Galambos guarantees, "Global oligopolies are as inevitable as the sunrise."[2] Ford Motor Company owns Aston Martin, Jaguar, and Volvo and has a controlling interest in Mazda. In 1998 there were forty car companies in the world. We will not be surprised to see only ten major survivors by 2008.

The globe is the final frontier of business consolidation. Worldwide airlines, energy and fuel companies, car manufacturers, pharmaceutical, and telecommunications firms are now joining together in a final flurry of combination that will continue through the next decade. The firm that emerges the winner during this next global consolidation contest will be positioned to win for many more decades into the future. While mergers and acquisitions will continue to be a focal point for the press, consolidation will, as we have described, take many forms of strategic alliances, joint ventures, cross-licensing, co-marketing, industry-wide consortia, and even cartels. Convergence of industries will also recast business consolidation into new forms. Even now, you can see an emerging consolidation trend that is blurring the lines between competitors and allies and changing the very definition of competition. In fact, the growth engine of the Internet—and its fastest growing firms—is fueled by co-investment among direct rivals. Even though both Microsoft and AOL have publicly proclaimed their fear of one another, they still enter into cooperative agreements as they pair-up to invest in many of the very same companies—like Roadrunner, a high-speed Internet cable business.

At the end of Chapter 5 we cited Denis Waitley's belief that leaders of the future will be champions of cooperation, not competition. *He is absolutely correct.* For example, while the entire world knows of the 1998 merger of Daimler-Benz and Chrysler, very few people are aware of a prior arrangement by which these same two companies were sharing vital resources since 1994. In an unusually cooperative connection between industry competitors, both Chrysler and Daimler-Benz produced cars in Magna International Inc.'s automotive manufacturing factory in Graz, Austria. For four years before the Daimler-Benz/Chrysler merger, Jeep Grand Cherokees, Chrysler Voyager minivans, Mercedes Benz G-class off-road vehicles and E-class sedans were all made in different sections of that same manufacturing facility. Both companies knew that cooperation through sharing the Graz facility would drive down total costs for both firms. Your team should give careful consideration to this crucial example, for it is the future model of collaborative growth. Jack Welch has coined the phrase "share to gain" to describe how GE collaborates with many others. In the current Exxon/Mobil oil merger, it is important to realize that both giant firms have numerous allied joint ventures with many direct competitors in most stages of their operations. For many firms in pharmaceuticals and telecommunications, these collaborative ventures are extremely common.

You may think that the Chrysler and Daimler-Benz arrangement was possible because of the lack of true head-to-head competition between their vehicles. But consider the cooperative deal struck between toe-to-toe market foes IBM and Dell Computer, first described in the Introduction. Because neither firm possessed 100 percent of the essential core competencies needed in the rapidly changing and consolidating world, both knew that "go it alone" strategy would not produce the best long-term results for either firm. By allying their strengths, together they plan to lead the pack in the crowded computer industry.

Additionally, Michael Dell may have been laying the foundation for a radical corporate transformation required for continued success into the twenty-first century. Dell knew that PCs were entering a plateau of market maturity, and might even decline. As early as the mid-1990s, technology experts were predicting the PC would be upstaged by so-called information appliances, simple devices that have

146

Info Appliances Will Outnumber Home PCs

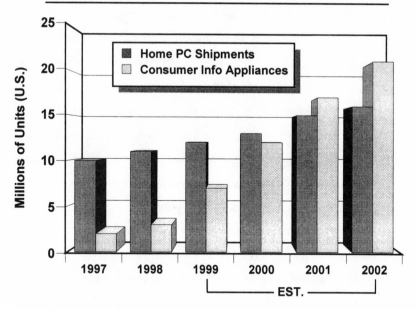

Source: International Data Corp.

much more specific functions than the "do everything" PC. These appliances matched some traditional household devices like the telephone, personal stereo, and television with low-power computer processors to create an all-new lineup of user-friendly gadgets. Newer technologies, like personal digital assistants, pocket electronic organizers, and vastly improved cellular phones were married with Internet and PC technology to provide users a much easier avenue to the Internet than the one provided by PCs. Many of the devices, like electronic books, digital picture frames, and wireless Internet "tablets," were newly designed and marketed to better serve consumers' needs using the very latest technologies. In early 1999 Sun Microsystems introduced its Jini software to allow any "smart" machine to communicate with any other. In short, the days of the PC as the key technology device and the main avenue to the Internet are numbered. Michael Dell will be ready.

The business landscape is exploding with breathtaking innovations, and it will only continue to grow in complexity and competitiveness. As a result, the skills you need to lead your team, department, division, or company must also become more and more comprehensive, flexible, and complex. For your firm to win in the consolidating world, you must become a *complete manager.* Your firm can *only* survive its journey through the land mines of failed mergers and brutal industry consolidation if your team understands and keeps perfecting a true and updated panoramic perspective of the world—with all its hidden traps and dangers but also its enormous wealth of untapped opportunities. Only when you can view the entire array of strategic opportunities through the simultaneous vision of a microscope and a powerful telescope can you place your firm in the optimal position for long-term success.

We have spelled out in detail our comprehensive lineup of consolidation strategies and tools specifically to help you become a more complete manager. You and your team need to understand that the overwhelming power of the consolidating world can both harm and help you, and you need to be able to craft winning strategies to help your company leap past industry competitors using the many practical and successful options we have presented here. Your strategies become the facets of your diamond. Like an expert diamond cutter, when you craft each facet of your composite strategy to work with all others to squeeze the most brilliance from your overall plan, you will profit by consolidation—both yours and your competitors'.

Appendix A

Largest Announced Transactions, 1999

U.S. TARGETS

	Target	Target Country	Acquirer	Acquirer Country	Value
1.	Sprint Corp.	US	MCI WorldCom	US	$127,274*
2.	Warner-Lambert Co.	US	Pfizer Inc.	US	87,947
3.	AirTouch Communications	US	Vodafone Group PLC	UK	65,902
4.	MediaOne Group Inc.	US	AT&T Corp.	US	63,115
5.	US WEST Inc.	US	Qwest Communications Inc.	US	48,480
6.	CBS Corp.	US	Viacom Inc.	US	40,882
7.	ARCO	US	BP Amoco PLC	UK	33,702
8.	Pharmacia & Upjohn Inc.	US	Monsanto Co.	US	26,772
9.	AMFM Inc.	US	Clear Channel Communications	US	21,819
10.	Ascend Communications Inc	US	Lucent Technologies Inc.	US	21,070
11.	Unicom Corp.	US	PECO Energy Co.	US	17,218
12.	Agilent Technologies Inc.	US	Shareholders	US	16,150
13.	BankBoston Corp.	US	Fleet Financial Group Inc.	US	15,925
14.	Honeywell Inc.	US	AlliedSignal Inc.	US	15,496
15.	Vodafone AirTouch	US	Bell Atlantic-Wireless Ops.	US	14,980

Appendix A

EUROPEAN TARGETS

	Target	Target Country	Acquirer	Acquirer Country	Value
1.	Mannesmann AG	Ger	Vodafone AirTouch PLC	UK	$148,616*
2.	Elf Aquitaine	Fra	Total Fina SA	Fra	58,811
3.	National Westminster Bank PLC	UK	Royal Bank of Scotland Group	UK	42,730
4.	Orange PLC	UK	Mannesmann AG	Ger	35,320
5.	Telecom Italia (IT Treasury)	Ita	Ing C Olivetti & Co. SpA	Ita	34,758
6.	Hoechst AG	Ger	Rhône-Poulenc SA	Fra	28,526
7.	Promodes	Fra	Carrefour SA	Fra	17,505
8.	VIAG AG	Ger	VEBA AG	Ger	16,275
9.	One 2 One	UK	Deutsche Telekom AG	Ger	13,629
10.	Paribas SA	Fra	BNP	Fra	13,201
11.	CWC Consumer Co.	UK	NTL Inc.	US	12,984
12.	Marconi Electronic Systems	UK	British Aerospace PLC	UK	12,863
13.	Banca Commerciale Italiana SpA	Ita	Banca Intesa SpA	Ita	12,791
14.	BOC Group PLC	UK	Investor Group	Fra	12,727
15.	INA	Ita	Assicurazioni Generali SpA	Ita	12,629

REMAINDER OF THE WORLD

	Target	Target Country	Acquirer	Acquirer Country	Value
1.	Dai-Ichi Kangyo Bank Ltd.	Jap	Fuji Bank Ltd.	Jap	$40,097*
2.	Industrial Bank of Japan Ltd.	Jap	Fuji Bank Ltd.	Jap	30,760
3.	YPF SA	Arg	Repsol SA	Spa	17,437
4.	KDD Corp.	Jap	DDI Corp.	Jap	14,080
5.	IDO Corp.	Jap	DDI Corp.	Jap	10,659
6.	Imasco Ltd.	Can	British American Tobacco PLC	UK	7,145
7.	Japan Leasing Corp.	Jap	General Electric Capital Corp.	US	6,566
8.	Fujian Mobile, Henan Mobile	PRC	China Telecom Hong Kong Ltd.	HK	6,398
9.	Canadian National . Railway Co	Can	Burlington Northern Santa Fe	US	6,021
10.	Nissan Motor Co.	Jap	Renault SA	Fra	5,391
11.	CT Financial Services Inc.	Can	TD Bank Financial Group	Can	5,303
12.	Bell Atlantic (BCE Inc.)	Can	Ameritech Corp.	US	3,383
13.	Cadillac Fairview Corp.	Can	Ontario Teachers' Pension Corp.	Can	3,290
14.	JDS Fitel (Furukawa Elec. Co.)	Can	Uniphase Corp.	US	3,058
15.	MacMillan Bioedel Ltd.	Can	Weyerhaeuser Co.	US	2,725

Source: J.P. Morgan Securities; transaction values computed by Securities Data Company

Note: In competing offers, only the higher offer (per SDC data) is included in all statistics

*$ in millions.

Global Cross-Region Transaction Trends, 1993–1999

U.S. & CANADA AND EUROPE

	U.S. & Canadian Target	European Target
1993	14	13
1994	39	15
1995	31	41
1996	51	32
1997	52	46
1998	198	79
1999	243	107

EUROPE AND ASIA/PACIFIC

	European Target	Asia/Pacific Target
1993	8	3
1994	2	2
1995	4	15
1996	4	14
1997	3	5
1998	12	14
1999	4	27

U.S. & CANADA AND ASIA/PACIFIC

	U.S. & Canadian Target	Asia/Pacific Target
1993	2	3
1994	2	2
1995	11	12
1996	8	7
1997	10	15
1998	4	21
1999	22	32

EUROPE AND LATIN AMERICA

	European Target	Latin American Target
1993	0	1
1994	0	4
1995	0	3
1996	0	6
1997	0	29
1998	0	29
1999	2	34

U.S. & CANADA AND LATIN AMERICA

	U.S. & Canadian Target	Latin American Target
1993	1	4
1994	1	4
1995	2	4
1996	1	9
1997	1	13
1998	0	23
1999	7	11

Source: J.P. Morgan Securities

*$ in billions

Comprehensive Research Summary of 29 Studies of Mergers and Acquisitions Completed from 1950 to 1999

Researcher(s)	Study	Summary of Findings
KPMG International, 1999[1]	700 of the most expensive deals from 1996 to 1998.	83% failed to boost shareholder wealth. 53 percent reduced shareholder wealth.
Saikat Chaudhuri and Behnam Tabrizi, 1999[2]	24 high-tech companies in their execution of 53 acquisitions	11 were considered successful by both sides; nine were clear failures; the remaining 33 provided zero or slightly positive but disappointing returns on investment.
Arthur Andersen Consulting, 1999[3]	All large mergers completed between 1994 and 1997	44% fell short of financial and strategic expectations. 70% of oil mergers didn't achieve the benefits they sought to accomplish.
Mark Sirower, 1999[4]	100 large deals from 1994 to 1997	2/3 of the deals met with negative market reactions and for the most part remained under-performers a year later.
Right Management Consultants, 1999[5]	179 merging companies	Fewer than 1/3 say they had successfully combined cultures.
Hay Group, 1999[5]	65 mergers	75% failed to place employees in the right roles in the first six months after merging.

Researcher(s)	Study	Summary of Findings
Daimler-Benz, 1998[6]	A Daimler study of cross-border combinations	70% of all cross-border mergers fail to thrive.
J.P. Morgan, 1998[7]	116 acquisitions of $1 billion + by European companies since 1985	44% added no value after three years.
A.T. Kearney, 1998[7]	115 mergers from 1993 to 1996	58% did not add value.
Kenneth W. Smith, 1997–8	215 transactions valued at $500 million + during the 1980s and 1990s	The 1990s deals achieved above industry returns only 52% of the time. 1980s deals faired even worse: 37%. Found that performance was related more to post-merger management than to strategy or price.
Healy, Palepu and Ruback, 1997	50 largest U.S. industrial takeovers from 1979 to mid-1984	Strategic takeovers, generally friendly transactions involving firms in overlapping businesses generated substantial gains for acquires. Hostile transactions between firms in unrelated businesses broke even at best.
Mark L. Sirower, 1997	168 mergers from 1979 to 1990	Average returns declined by 20% four years after the deal.
Tim Loughran and Anand Vijh, 1997	Compared stock, cash, and "combination" deals of 947 acquisitions between 1970 and 1989	Stock acquisitions earned significantly negative returns versus cash acquisitions.
Coopers & Lybrand, 1996	125 companies during their post-merger period	66% were financially unsuccessful. Found correlation between a slow pace of post-merger transition and low levels of revenue, cash flow and profitability.
David Birch, 1996	Compared acquirers versus nonacquirers among 13 million enterprises in the U.S. between 1992 and 1995	Only 60% of acquirers generate significant growth in net income following their purchases when compared to nonacquirers.
David Mitchell, 1996	A survey of 150 acquisitive companies	70% of all acquisitions fail to meet the expectations of their architects.

Researcher(s)	Study	Summary of Findings
Ira Smolowitz and Clayton Hillyer, 1996	Studied 45 firms in the *Forbes* 500 to identify merger failure factors	In interviews, senior executives cited the major merger failure factors as: cultural incompatibility, clashing management styles and egos, inability to implement change, inability to forecast, and excessive optimism with regard to synergy.
Mercer Management Consulting and *Business Week,* 1995	Comparison of 248 acquirers that purchased 1,045 companies from 1990 to 1995 and 96 nonacquirers	69% of the nonacquirers produced better returns than the industry index. 58% of the acquirers produced better returns. Blamed post-merger failure on inadequate due diligence, lack of compelling strategy, overly optimistic expectations of synergy, conflicting corporate culture, and slow post-merger integration.
Mercer Management Consulting and *Business Week,* 1995	150 $500 million + deals from 1990 to 1995	17% created substantial returns for the acquirer, 33% created marginal returns, 20% eroded returns, and 30% substantially eroded returns to the shareholder relative to industry peers over three years.
Paul M. Healy, Krishma Palepu, and Richard S. Ruback, 1992	50 major deals between 1979 and 1984	Merged firms found significant improvements in asset productivity relative to their industries, leading to higher operating cash flow returns. These findings were particularly strong for transactions involving firms in overlapping businesses, suggesting that post-merger integration plays a role in post-merger value.
Phillippe C. Haspeslagh and David B. Jemison, 1991	Five-year study of 20 acquirers based in six countries making acquisitions in 10 countries	The most successful acquirers ensure both strategic and operational fit. The least successful ensure neither.

Appendix C

Researcher(s)	Study	Summary of Findings
Alok Chakrabarti, 1990	31 acquisitions	Post-merger performance depends more on post-merger integration than on strategy.
American Management Association, late 1980's[9]	54 big mergers	50% led to reduced productivity, profits, or both.
PA Consulting of London, 1989	28 major acquisitions in U.S. banking from 1982 to 1988	80% of acquisitions have a negative impact on the acquirer's share price.
Michael Bradley, Anand Desai, and E. Han Kim, 1987	236 tender offers completed between 1963 and 1984	Stock market responses to announcements of completed mergers bring positive returns (+7.43% average) to shareholders of both bidding and target firms.
Michael Porter, 1987[8]	3,788 acquisitions by 33 leading U.S. companies from 1950 to 1986	Acquired companies were divested at a rate that ranged from over 50% to 74%.
McKinsey & Co., 1987[9]	116 acquisitions	77% did not cover the costs incurred in the deal. 61% failed to earn back equity capital invested within three years.
Malcolm S. Salter and Wolf A. Weinhold, 1979	36 companies that grew through mergers	Average return on equity for the firms was 44% below average NYSE levels. Average return on assets was 75% below NYSE.
Johan Brjokstan, 1965	5,409 manufacturing mergers from 1955 to 1965	866 of the mergers failed financially, strategically, and/or technologically.

Source: All studies are cited in Alexandra Reed Lajoux and J. Fred Weston, "Do Deals Deliver on Post-Merger Performance?" *Mergers & Acquisitions*, September/October 1998, pp. 34–37, except:

1. Nikhil Deogun, "Merger Wave Spurs More Stock Wipeouts," *The Wall Street Journal*, November 29, 1999, p. C1.

2. Saikat Chaudhuri and Behnam Tabrizi, "Capturing the Real Value in High-Tech Acquisitions," *Harvard Business Review*, September-August, 1999, p. 124.

3. Bhushan Bahree, "Oil Mergers Don't Live Up to the Hype," *The Wall Street Journal*, July 23, 1999, p. A10.

4. Mark L. Sirower, "What Acquiring Minds Need to Know," *The Wall Street Journal,* February 22, 1999, p. A18.

5. "Tight Fit: Merging Companies See Need to Find the Right Roles for Employees," *The Wall Street Journal,* February 16, 1999, p. A1.

6. Brian Coleman and Gregory L. White, "In High-Tech War Rooms, Giant Is Born," *The Wall Street Journal,* November 13, 1998, p. B1.

7. Jeffery L. Hiday, "Most Mergers Fail to Add Value, Consultants Find," *The Wall Street Journal,* October 12, 1998, p. B9I.

8. Michael E. Porter, "From Competitive Advantage to Corporate Strategy," *Harvard Business Review,* May–June, 1987, p. 45.

9. Anne B. Fisher, "How to Make a Merger Work," *Fortune,* January 24, 1994, p. 66.

Appendix D

Forces Driving Merger Waves

Given the overwhelming evidence that mergers fail with alarming regularity, then *why* do firms continue their unquenchable thirst to join together? Multiple forces, which have far more power than any compelling merger failure data from consultants and academics, continue to push companies together. These forces are powerful, unrelenting, and dynamic. Of critical importance, however, they are *real,* and companies succumb to them at ever increasing rates. The forces are many—some old as the dawn of modern business, some industry-specific, and some new. Others have yet to emerge.

The quest for giant size. The burning desire to build a bigger company has been constant for over 200 years. Many companies make acquisitions in order to become too big to be swallowed by a competitor firm and therefore secure their continued independence. In 1998 Fleet Financial Group's CEO Terrence Murray publicly announced he was shopping for acquisitions that would inject up to an additional $100 billion in assets to the banking company and ensure its independence in the rapidly converging banking market.[1]

In a few short months, Fleet had acquired the commercial finance unit of Sanwa Bank Ltd., a specialist operation from Merrill Lynch, and credit card receivables from Household International. Murray noted, "We're probably not fully there." His ultimate goal was to buy an independence insurance policy by accumulating between $150 billion and $200 billion in total assets.[2] In 1999 the potential final piece of Fleet's puzzle was announced—a $16 billion acquisition of BankBoston Corp. Having now amassed $180 billion in assets, Murray was convinced Fleet could stand alone. Industry analysts, however, in their never-ending desire to see bigger and bigger deals, weren't convinced—Fleet was still "just" the eighth largest bank in the United States.

The relentless drive for sales growth to meet the expectations of owners and shareholders. Managers are rewarded for their ability to grow a business. As a trend, flat sales never have been and never will be acceptable in any business. Investors demand ongoing increases in market share and geographic expansion to drive up revenue. They drive the "bigger is better" syndrome.

This drive for revenue growth has become known as "strategic bigness." Many managers and shareholders are convinced that in order to become a credible player in a global market, sales measured in billions will always beat those measured in millions. While smaller firms can no doubt flourish in an ever-expanding territory, size often gives an illusion of strength to both customers and suppliers. Profitability often takes a back seat to revenue. While size may provide opportunities for purchasing discounts and other benefits, size on its own will in no way guarantee financial success. You can look back to Chapter 3 and the Boeing story for a graphic reminder.

The oldest consolidation motivator. The oldest of all motivators—*fear*—still plays a pivotal role. Fear has been a catalyst in every merger wave, from the building of the national railroads in the 1800s to the proliferation of conglomerates in the 1980s to our current merger tidal wave. In the horse race to create the world standard for e-commerce, fear is an extremely rational emotion because the firm that wins by establishing the industry standard will prosper beyond all imagination. All firms who finish second or worse will be paying for the right to use the standard. It has become a brutal war zone involving both huge corporations and tiny start-ups, each trying to become the world's next Microsoft. They are all fighting for the chance to fuel explosive global growth by widely proliferating the use of their own technology standard while simultaneously eclipsing the proposed technologies of their competitors.

The drive for global reach. The motivation to claim global status has never been greater. True globalization of goods and services is the final frontier of geographic expansion. Within a generation, national consolidation has given way to cross-border consolidation which is now giving way to unprecedented cross-continent M&A activity in a host of industries.

Leapfrogging advances in technology. Technology advances, currently exemplified by the computer industry, biotech, and the Internet, have long been an underlying force driving consolidation and convergence of industries. Often these fusions were in industries that previously had little or no contact with one another. Also, technology advances are often born in the fertile grounds of academic

163

institutions. Many universities have had long-standing R&D cooperative agreements with a wide variety of industries.

Discoveries in one industry often lead to cascading reapplications
and discoveries in many industries. Exponential growth in technology is often matched by exponential growth in consolidation.
Netscape CEO James Barksdale, after agreeing to sell his thirty-
nine-month-old company to America Online in 1998, stated, "I
think industries, as they mature, consolidate."[3]

While technology advances start by creating new links between
businesses, these links often lead to combination opportunities.
Many firms seek to merge, acquire, or create various formal alliances with others to ensure they have access to the best technologies to ensure future success. Their technical expertise builds their
competitive capability to survive in the continually reinvented competitive landscape. A firm's technical skill set must enable it to compete with its market opponents who are also on a never-ending
technology hunt.

The need to make significant investments in new technology. Jim
Dixon, president of technology and operations for NationsBank
Corp. stated that new technology was the "fuel" that was driving
bank consolidation.[4] When a bank needs to upgrade a complicated,
expensive technology like the sophisticated computer systems, au-
tomatic teller machines, networks, telephone, and online, customer-
driven transaction capabilities that are now standard in the banking
industry, it may be economically more attractive to merge with a
competitor who already has the newest technology than to upgrade.

Terrence Larsen, chairman of CoreStates Financial Corp., estimated that year 2000 computer upgrades alone would cost his bank close to $60 million. During merger discussions with First Union in 1997, he learned that bringing CoreStates systems up to speed with First Union's year 2000 compatible system would cost only $10 million. He used this information as part of his decision to agree to a takeover by First Union.[5]

Retirement, no heirs, or no willing heirs to assume leadership in a closely held business. Small business owners have long faced the challenge of how to best turn over their business when there is no suitable nor willing family member to take the reins. Across the globe, bicycle shops, bakeries, and printers have sold out to new owners when it came time to retire. Often they sell to another owner in the same industry who is growing through acquisition. In fact, only 39 percent of family-owned businesses in the United States survive to the second generation.[6]

Larger companies can face this same challenge. When George Bunting, Noxell Corporation chairman, majority shareholder, and grandson of the founder, decided to sell the family business to Procter & Gamble in 1988, he had no heirs willing to take the reins of his leading U.S. mass market cosmetics company. Rather than to continue his ownership but allow the business to run without the family at the helm, Bunting opted to accept P&G's generous offer of $1.3 billion.

Technology force—where you may least expect it. From the invention of the steam engine to the transistor to the microprocessor, technological advances create consolidation. The microprocessor alone is bringing together firms who were strangers just a few years ago. Manufacturers of jet engines and hospital diagnostic equipment reside comfortably within one corporation. While technology drives high-tech consolidation, it can also present a major force in industries where you would least expect it—even marketers of children's building blocks have allied with academic engineering think tanks to create new products. One of the most productive combinations in the toy industry to date has resulted in Denmark's Lego Group *Mindstorm* robot.

Through an intense collaborative venture with the Massachusetts Institute of Technology, Lego has produced a high-tech masterpiece. Each *Mindstorm* set includes Lego's trademark interlocking blocks, a palm-sized microcomputer, light and touch sensors, and an infrared communication link to the microcomputer that allows the owner to download programming directly from his or her personal computer. The robot can be built and programmed to play tag or even announce when the mail is delivered. The techno-hungry public loved it. First-year demand was so great that Lego was forced to bump its U.S. sales forecast by 567 percent.[7] The consolidation of computers and toys is so promising, even microprocessor giant Intel Corp. didn't want to be left out of the toy chest—in early 1999 it joined with Mattel Inc. to develop a totally new line of interactive toys.

Every business, *high-tech or not,* has the ability to match its products and services with another firm's products and services to create something new. Because the inventive world becomes exponentially more inventive, the potential combinations are infinite. This most certainly means more mergers and acquisitions, but even those firms who cannot or will not enter the merger game can still reap the benefits of expanded resources, technologies, or research. Many variations of collaborations, strategic alliances, and joint ventures can readily meet their needs to expand their resource base.

Soaring stock market. The last half of the 1990s saw stock valuations and corporate market capitalization rise to ever increasing new records. It also saw the greatest level of stock used as "currency" to finance acquisitions. Stock swaps were the transaction method of choice during the consolidations of the 1990s. Thirteen of the fifteen largest mergers in 1998 were completed through stock swaps.

Many acquirers were duped into a false sense of new wealth based on the dizzying levels of their stock prices and market capitalization. This is a dangerous trap. While the raging bull market

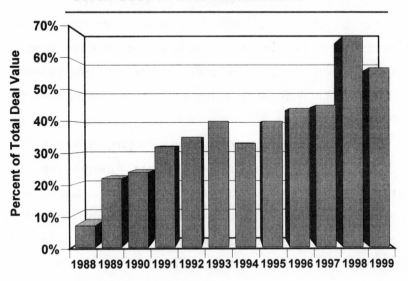

Stock Used in U.S. Transactions

Source: J.P. Morgan Securities

drives up the acquirer's stock, at the same time it drives up the cost of potential targets. This can create a cancellation effect: the new riches of the acquirer are often cancelled out by the new priceyness of the target. (Although a *falling* stock market, like that in the Spring of 2000, often drives interest *away* from troubled industries and regions, a plunging stock market can also *propel* mergers or acquisitions of bankrupt firms at bargain basement prices. GE Capital has seized opportunity in Asia in just this manner.)

Fear that the firm will be swept under in a quickly consolidating industry. Fear of being swept under is a classic "eat or be eaten" mentality. Small business owners in particular often have a "get in now or be buried alive" perspective. They fear they may not survive in what is becoming an industry of far fewer, but larger, participants. Lightning-fast roll-ups of highly fragmented local markets are particularly successful when this anxiety is present within an industry.

Holman Jenkins of *The Wall Street Journal* commented: "So behind today's merger frenzy lies cold fear. Technology is changing the way business is done, and managements are seizing these opportunities not with a song in their heart but in terror of being left behind."[8]

Even large companies, like the European pharmaceuticals, fear the growing strength and snowballing power of merging competitors. Within just seven days of Germany's Hoechst AG and France's Rhône-Poulenc SA announcement to create the world's largest pharmaceutical force, France's Sanofi SA and Synthelabo SA, and separately, the United Kingdom's Zeneca Group and Sweden's Astra unveiled their plans to join forces. European drug makers scrambled to grow larger both to give themselves a better chance of finding a desirable U.S. partner in the future and to develop more marketing clout.[9]

The need for people. In labor-short industries—like computer software—many acquisitions are driven by industry-wide shortages of human capital. Microsoft, for example, has frequently purchased small boutique software development firms. While they frequently acquired niche technology, the real target was often the firm's talented programmers and developers. In an industry where the product life is just eighteen months, the specific products are often just icing on the cake. The real prize is the gifted software executives and technical experts.

Hiring through acquisitions has become AT&T Corp. CEO Michael Armstrong's hiring method of choice. When Armstrong reorganized AT&T into two separate units in early 1999—business and consumer—he called upon acquired executives to run the show. Leo Hindery, from Tele-Communications Inc., and Robert Annunziata, from Teleport Communications Group, were tapped to run the two business units.

Personal gains for M&A decision makers. Executives of target companies are legally bound to serve the best interests of shareholders. However, they often receive huge personal windfall as a result of a merger. Ted Turner at Time Warner reaped a colossal financial windfall. On the very day America Online announced its acquisition of Time Warner, Turner's personal fortune soared by almost $3 billion. The acquisition of Bankers Trust Corp by Deutsche Bank AG made BT chairman and CEO Frank Newman one of the highest paid executives in the commercial banking industry. As part of his personal employment contract with Deutsche Bank, he agreed to stay with the merged organization for five years at a $900,000 per year salary—plus an annual bonus of $10.1 million. While we have no reason to believe post-merger financial arrangements played any part in these particular acquisitions, you can see how personal fortunes can be affected by an M&A transaction.

Falling prices of goods or services. The failure of the OPEC cartel to keep oil prices artificially high in 1997 and 1998 led to a rash of price cuts and fierce competition in the world oil industry. By the latter part of 1998 oil prices plunged 30 percent from the previous year and were dangerously close to a twelve-year low.[10] Revenues flat-lined and oil producers rushed to the merger table. They had to make a move to bring costs into line with the lower prices they were receiving for their gas and oil, so they turned to mergers. In the second half of 1998 alone there were four different combinations, highlighted by the mega-mergers of British Petroleum and Amoco and then Exxon and Mobil.

Changes in government laws. Just as governments can stop mergers and acquisitions, they can be a major driving force of consolidation—and currently, the walls of political and national protectionism are falling at a staggering rate. National laws, geographic boundaries, and financial protectionism are all undergoing radical transformations in countries throughout the world. Broad-reaching political and social changes, like the end of the Cold War, opened borders and markets that for years had been shut more securely than a bank vault. Additionally, specific government legislation—like the U.S. Telecommunications Act of 1996—made the potential reconnection of the Baby Bells SBC and Ameritech and then Bell Atlantic and GTE a real possibility.

The North American Free Trade Agreement (NAFTA) and the European Economic Union have both opened doors previously closed to cross-border merger partners. NAFTA created a profusion of Mexican acquisitions by foreign partners, from banks and tobacco companies to makers of tequila bottles and even Mexico's most famous brewery.[11] When the euro started trading in January 1999, it was the final step to slash transaction costs and foster cross-border partnerships in Europe. Consolidation of all forms could be entered into without the fear of financial risk brought about by fluctuating national currencies. In one stroke, the euro's launch erased most of Europe's monetary borders. Almost overnight, the European Economic Union created an economic force with a market the size of the United States. Cross-border and cross-continent mergers, acquisitions, and all forms of alliances exploded starting in late 1998 and early 1999.

Overcapacity or shrinking demand for the industry's goods or services. With the sweeping changes in the U.S. health care industry, the amount of hospital time patients spend for specific medical procedures or illnesses is shrinking. Managed care insurers are demanding shorter and shorter stays as their key target to drive down costs. "Patient days" are expected to drop by an additional 25 percent in the next five years.[12]

This change has been a tough financial slap to hospitals because empty beds generate costs but no revenue. In the Baltimore hospital

171

market alone, eight major hospitals have responded by creating four different alliances or mergers. This will help them consolidate the in-patient services portion of their facilities and allow for a reduction of many beds while still meeting occupancy demand levels. By then boosting occupancy *rates,* the merged hospitals hope to drive down costs and redirect enough money to offer new services.

In the United States, the defense industry reeled from a six-year spell of frenetic M&A activity from 1993 to 1998. The role of government in jump-starting consolidation has never been so blatant nor forceful. The federal government is virtually the sole customer for the entire industry, and because defense purchases were falling to record low levels, the Pentagon knew it could not support the existing lineup of contractors. The Justice Department readily endorsed combinations that created near-monopoly power—but they had no other reasonable choice if they didn't want to see their suppliers fall into bankruptcy. So market-dominating combinations were approved and three giants emerged—Boeing, Lockheed, and Raytheon.

However, the government gives and the government takes away. In the summer of 1998 the Justice Department decided they had seen enough of the big contractor combination and squelched a proposed Lockheed Martin–Northrop Grumman merger. Both the Justice Department and the Pentagon still wanted to see more consolidation, but not at the mega-merger level. Instead, they provided up-front encouragement to smaller contractors like TRW (satellite payloads), Alliant Techsystems (rocket motors), and Cordant Technologies (solid propulsion systems). Defense Secretary William Cohen stated, "We intend to support future mergers and consolidations, certainly at the second and third tier levels."[13]

Additionally, the automotive world has experienced rampant consolidation among firms of all sizes during the last three years. In the twelve months before the headline-grabbing DaimlerChrysler $38 billion deal in 1998, the global automotive industry had been forced into more than seven hundred mergers and acquisitions totaling $28 billion. London's *Financial Times* reported the consolidation was driven by "global over-capacity and poor prospects for growth."[14] Within days of the DaimlerChrysler announcement, Chrysler chairman Robert Eaton told the press that he knew of six other sets of negotiation between car makers.[15] "With the world economy in the situation it is, and the fact that only about 10 out of the 40 manufacturers in the world are making money, there's going to be a dramatic restructuring. Everybody's talking to everybody in the auto industry."[16] Within a few months, it was no surprise when Ford announced its acquisition of Volvo.

Core business transformation. Many companies combine with others, acquire, or sell parts of their existing business to literally change industries within which they conduct business. Westinghouse's former CEO Michael Jordan purchased CBS with the goal of completely transforming the core business. He simultaneously dismantled the storied industrial conglomerate and rebuilt it with broadcasting acquisitions. By buying CBS, a cable television network, and Infinity Broadcasting Co., and systematically razing the hodgepodge of "old" Westinghouse businesses, Jordan fabricated a completely new company. He divested Westinghouse divisions, including stalwarts defense and power generation, one by one.

From 1994 to 1998 Jordan sold Distribution and Controls, The

Knoll Group (office furniture), Defense Electronics, Thermo King (refrigeration equipment), Westinghouse Energy Systems, and Westinghouse Government Operations.[17] Jordan created a totally different, totally new Westinghouse. What had been a long-standing giant in industrial machinery, consumer durables, defense, and energy was now a media powerhouse. His final step in the transformation was to change the company moniker to a name that better reflected its new industry position—*CBS!*[18]

The reasons to enter the combination game are endless. Some firms combine in response to customer pressures to develop more capability or capacity. In particular, law firms have had to combine to meet the demands of their clients. As more and more companies operate on a national basis—like banks—they want a relationship with very few law firms—not a different one in every city or region where they do business. Many law firms have joined together through mergers and acquisitions to quickly establish their presence in multiple cities. This same force is leading to a coming wave of *global* law mergers and alliances.

Jack Welch at GE buys and sells companies and business units with great regularity—all in order to position each business to meet his rigorous criteria as being number one or two in each respective industry. If GE cannot be first or second, it exits that market. While this central strategy has resulted in many acquisitions, it has also seen several divestitures. In the 1980s GE divested $10 billion worth of what they termed "marginal" businesses.[19] Other CEOs are simply driven by ego. They feel compelled to land a big acquisition or merger to leave their mark on the organization—after all, with

174

everyone else on the merger bandwagon, they don't want posterity to remember them as the CEO who couldn't swing a big deal.

Finally, others join together in a pure play for synergy. They are convinced (with a little assistance from their investment bankers), that there are market opportunities, cost savings, or operational improvements that will *only* be discovered through consolidation. They hope for the elusive $1 + 1 = 3$ equation. This all too often proves to be only a shell game.

———————

The underlying reasons and motivations for companies, their executives and owners to consolidate are far-reaching, varied, and unique to each situation. Your understanding of the key consolidation forces, whether it be merger, acquisition, strategic alliance, or joint venture, will help you to win in the consolidating world. The more you understand about both yourself and your competitors, the better you will be able to craft the right strategies to win in your specific competitive arena.

Boeing's Blunder

J ust weeks after completing its acquisition of Rockwell's defense operations, Boeing announced its plan to purchase McDonnell Douglas, catapulting Boeing into far and away the world's largest aerospace company. The new Boeing would outsell its nearest defense competitor, Lockheed Martin, by $18 billion each year. Industry experts said that Boeing's expertise in building commercial aircraft combined with McDonnell Douglas's team of fighter (aircraft) experts should leave Lockheed Martin "undoubtedly very scared."[1] It would own the commercial aircraft market because Boeing forecasted that it would be producing 65 percent of the world's airliners versus 35 percent for Airbus Industrie, the European consortium from France, Germany, the United Kingdom and Spain.

Top officials from Boeing and McDonnell Douglas could hardly contain their glee about the combination. Boeing CEO Philip Condit called the transaction "an historic moment in aviation and aerospace." McDonnell Douglas Chairman John McDonnell was even more glowing, proclaiming the new Boeing would be the "largest, strongest, broadest, most admired aerospace company in the world."[2]

But the merger was grounded from the start. Little did both men realize that they were systematically taking all the steps necessary to force Boeing into its greatest business free-fall ever. Boeing would lose world market dominance in its highly visible and previously profitable commercial airliner business and post a net operating loss *for the very first time in fifty years.*

Analysts thought the new Boeing had a stranglehold on the throats of its two remaining competitors—Lockheed and Airbus. No one, either inside or outside Boeing, was ready for the series of disasters that would follow within the next months and bring Boeing to its knees. Boeing overwhelmingly, stunningly, and naively failed to understand the great amount of time, energy, and effort required to integrate the operations of Rockwell and McDonnell Douglas. They timed the acquisitions to coincide with a comprehensive overhaul of their antiquated, fifty-year-old production process, the introduction of the next-generation 737 aircraft, plus a planned 132 percent increase in total production output. Their hoped for goal of both mergers was market dominance and financial success. Instead, however, the near total chaos of Boeing's two giant corporate takeovers caused an interrelated series of disastrous sales, production, global forecasting, and merger integration snafus that resulted in overwhelming success for their lone commercial airline competitor—Airbus.

When Boeing completed the McDonnell Douglas acquisition in August 1997, Boeing stock was trading at a near all-time high and demand for commercial aircraft was booming. How daunting was the challenge Boeing had created for itself? Let's first explore the production process Boeing was determined to fix. That process was more than broken.[3] Boeing was still using the engineering, manufacturing, and purchasing systems that had been in place since the days of their WWII B-17 and B-29 bombers. During manufacturing, every part of every plane was still being tracked manually. As computers were introduced to help manage data, each and every department developed and maintained its own data base, including parts lists. These almost four hundred data bases, of course, could not effectively talk to one another.

Not unlike a busy local car repair shop, Boeing's workers swarmed over its planes, each person completing a seemingly independent set of tasks. The work is surprisingly low tech—most of it completed with hand tools. Boeing's production system needed 216 workers for each aircraft produced in a year—far less efficient than the 143 workers needed at Airbus.[4]

Boeing's selling system also allowed customers free rein to order any modifications to suit their needs and whims. This order modification system included important choices (like the brand of engine) and ridiculous options like the location of emergency flashlights, cockpit clipboard features, and placement of heating and cooling ducts.

Boeing had taken some timid steps since the 1970s to fix this archaic system, but they really didn't attempt to make any substantial, lasting, systematic changes. They finally started in earnest in 1994 to streamline the production operation. One of their goals was to place severe limits on plane configurations so that customers would not have free choice of meaningless options. They also wanted to replace the proliferation of existing computer systems with just four new ones—four that could actually communicate with one another. And the computers would share a single parts list for each plane.

179

So Boeing launched its "nose-to-tail" manufacturing overhaul in 1994. Dubbed "DCAC/MRM," even the program name reflected the lumbering bureaucracy of old. And if everything progressed as designed, the transformation wouldn't be in place until the next century. The plans for building planes in a whole new way were comprehensive and daunting. What a tremendously *wrong* time to integrate two new acquisitions!

Not only did Boeing choose this particular time for acquisitions, they also made plans to more than double normal monthly production output from 18.5 to 43 planes. Demand for commercial airliners was going through the roof and Boeing's sales organization couldn't resist the temptation to promise the moon without matching orders with the capability of the production system to deliver.

The very idea that a smooth, brand-new total production transformation and a doubling of output could be accomplished simultaneously in less than two years is difficult to comprehend. To believe that both could be accomplished within the same time frame as merger integration with two major corporations, Rockwell and McDonnell Douglas, was nothing short of sheer madness.

However, Boeing's corporate nightmare involved even more obstacles. Parts suppliers could not keep up with increased demand because industry-wide consolidation had resulted in fewer machining facilities to supply critical components. Any glitch in the ability to deliver components (like a shortage of titanium, a critical aircraft alloy) caused Boeing's planes to be built out of sequence. Planes often sat waiting for parts to complete one step of the process before other steps could be started.

But what made this aerospace giant's trouble even worse was that

Boeing had simultaneously signed enormous, very long-term and potentially money-losing deals with three major airline carriers. They negotiated twenty-year contracts to lock in exclusive rights to supply aircraft to Delta, American, and Continental. If the airlines exercise all the options in these contracts, they will buy planes only from Boeing for two entire decades. The surprising downside and huge financial risk, however, was that Boeing had entered into a fierce bidding war with Airbus to win these contracts. As the bidding against Airbus became more savage, Boeing had to discount their planes by 20 percent to win the long-term exclusive agreements. Additionally, Boeing agreed to pay expensive financial penalties to these carriers and others if they failed to deliver the new planes on rigidly fixed time schedules. Conventional wisdom would have you believe the Boeing-Airbus duopoly could control their destiny. Instead, they fell into a bidding war trap set by the airline carriers.

In a nutshell, Boeing was simultaneously reinventing their process for making planes, more than doubling capacity, taking far more orders than they could deliver, and digesting two giant corporate acquisitions—*simultaneously.* To further complicate Boeing's self-imposed dilemma, the Far East (where most of Boeing's profits from the 747 huge cash cow is derived) was entering into its now famous Asian financial crisis. Boeing was doomed to fail—their near-monopoly consolidation strategy was creating their biggest financial disaster ever. Their acquisition strategy was ill-planned, ill-timed, and ill-executed. They handed a double-edged sword to Airbus.

How great was the impact on Boeing? Pierre Chao of Morgan Stanley Dean Witter calculated that Boeing's gross inventories ballooned to $18 billion, about 35 percent of total revenues. Production problems on both the 747 and new-generation 737 lines become so great that Boeing was forced to tell customers they could not deliver planes when promised. By autumn 1997 the out-of-sequence problems were worsening. The 747 line was running more than fourteen thousand jobs out of sequence or behind schedule.[5] (Three thousand or fewer out of sequence is considered manageable.) Overtime costs skyrocketed.

The botched merger integration of McDonnell Douglas and Rockwell threw jet fuel onto the fire. Boeing executives had placed many critical integration issues on the back burner. They still had not resolved such fundamental topics such as which factories would remain open, which products would be discontinued, and who would report to whom.[6]

Merger integration must start even before the announcement of a merger. When no advance planning is done, and when integration is not conducted on a fast-track schedule, total chaos, uncertainty, and worker anxiety are guaranteed. Boeing executives failed to understand the impact of a poorly conducted merger integration. *It cannot be delayed.* Boeing made the mistake of plowing ahead with production transformation and capacity increase programs at the expense of the merger integration. Merger integration issues do not lie quietly dormant while other issues are being addressed. They demand breakthrough planning, effort, determination, and conviction. When the issues of integrating two organization's people, systems, and operations are left unattended, they are swiftly churned into an amazing tangle of emotions, misunderstandings, and chaos. Boeing will be repairing damage from their many unplanned merger integration mistakes for years to come.

On September 29, 1997, production problems had become so gravely tangled that Ronald Woodward, president of Boeing's Commercial Airplane Group, ordered a production stop of both the 747 and 737 lines. He dejectedly reasoned that stopping, regrouping, and finishing the backlog of partially completed planes was the only way to climb out of the abyss.

Boeing's financial and market losses have cut deep. Boeing has been forced to write off $4 billion due to its operational problems. From August 1997 to the last days of 1998 Boeing stock dropped from 60 to 29, resulting in a loss of shareholder wealth of almost $31 billion.[7]

By mid-summer 1998 Boeing's commercial airliner market share had eroded to 48 percent, literally handing Airbus the majority of the business. Will Boeing bounce back? Probably. But not without suffering further damage. In July 1998 Boeing was dealt another setback as US Airways ordered its first wide-body airlines—from Airbus.

Then in September, thirty-year Boeing veteran Ron Woodward resigned under pressure and was replaced by Alan Mulally as head of jetliner production and sales. By then, Boeing had finally come to grips with reality and acknowledged the impact of Asia's economic problems. They announced sharp reductions in their output plans by cutting forecasts for every jetliner model. The resulting personnel reduction would total 48,000 by the end of 2000.

Boeing's self-inflicted wounds continued to plague the aerospace giant well into 2000. Because any labor strike would further cripple the company, the machinist union was able to negotiate an extremely favorable contract for its members. Boeing was forced to concede to union demands because the union held all the negotiating power. They knew Boeing simply couldn't survive a lengthy strike. The engineering and technical worker union, however, did strike in early 2000, causing serious delays in Boeing's delivery of new aircraft. In late February, only four planes had been delivered, compared to forty-seven in the same month of 1999.

And finally, the Federal Aviation Administration announced it would conduct a "special evaluation" of Boeing's jetliner production system.[8] Production problems (ranging from improperly fastened tail section bolts to excess glue application that increased flammability potential beyond federal standards to a tool left behind in a jet fuel tank) were becoming alarmingly common on Boeing assembly lines. The FAA had lost confidence in Boeing's ability to meet federal aviation production standards. The audit may well result in fines or production disruptions. Boeing's blunders continue to haunt this former world leader.

Appendix F

Al Dunlap's Demise

The recent demise of Al Dunlap at Sunbeam Corporation was the direct result of a simultaneous purchase and fumbling of three different businesses—Coleman Co., First Alert, and Signature Brands. Dunlap was so preoccupied with his triple takeover he made fatal sales, marketing, and operational blunders in Sunbeam's own businesses. Revenues plunged and Al literally "chainsawed" shareholder wealth. Sunbeam's stock price was at a fifty-two-week high when Dunlap announced the acquisitions. In less than four months, it plunged over 84 percent. Sunbeam was a perfect target for strategic attacks.

Dunlap's expertise is clearly rooted in his ability to turn around ailing companies. Even with his well documented "finesse," Dunlap's track record of cutting costs and increasing shareholder wealth has been nothing short of stellar. At Sunbeam, Dunlap applied the same formula that worked so well for him at Lily-Tulip, Crown-Zellerbach, and Scott Paper. He stormed in, fired half of Sunbeam's employees, sold off non-core businesses, and closed numerous facilities, including sixteen of twenty-six factories, five of six headquarters and forty-three of sixty-one warehouses.[1]

Wall Street cheered and Sunbeam's stock rocketed from 12 to 49 in just eighteen months. While the stock price increase delighted shareholders, it also spelled disaster for Sunbeam as a takeover target. Dunlap's normal process was to slash, burn, and then sell. Sunbeam's market capitalization surged to over $3.4 billion, making it an expensive takeover choice as it had only about $1 billion in revenue and was locked in a slow growth industry. No other firm was willing to buy and Dunlap was forced to assess other options.

However, just as so many before him, he grossly underestimated the obstacles in his path. Even as he was working deals to acquire Coleman, First Alert, and Signature Brands, Dunlap started losing both sight and control of Sunbeam's core businesses. His unrelenting attacks to drive out costs ultimately led employees to make some very damaging high-risk decisions. They gave big quantity price discounts to the trade in "receive now, pay later" bargains designed to inflate revenue, but the deals only led to quick profit erosion. *Barron's* reported that accounting "gimmickry" artificially boosted 1997 profits.[2] At first Sunbeam cried, "Foul," but later sheepishly admitted that 1997 financial statements "should not be relied upon."[3]

When Dunlap announced his $2.5 billion triple-play acquisition in March 1998, Sunbeam stock was trading at an all time high of $53. From the very day of the announcement, it started its steep freefall. Two critical issues became very apparent. First, Dunlap's foray into complex multiple deal-making as an acquirer required far more time and in-depth attention than he ever imagined. Dunlap failed to heed the advice about the power of organization focus that he himself had offered in his book *Mean Business:* "But executives and boards don't want to hear about becoming a smaller company. They think bigger is better, which isn't true."[4]

Second, he severely miscalculated the impact of simultaneously bringing together four previously separate companies. Sunbeam was already a bare-bones operation due to Dunlap's slash and burn program. Before Dunlap, Sunbeam had been a $1 billion company with twelve thousand employees. Now it was a $1 billion company with six thousand employees. This same skeleton crew could not successfully integrate its people, systems, and operations with three other newly acquired companies. The acquisition process is an incredibly taxing undertaking in even the best circumstances. The turmoil finally exploded when Ron Perelman, now a major Sunbeam shareholder after agreeing to sell his huge majority stake in Coleman, squared off with Dunlap about how best to transition the Coleman acquisition. Was there chaos at Sunbeam? Undoubtedly. Very few managers have ever accurately estimated the difficulty of integrating companies after an acquisition or merger. "Chainsaw" Al Dunlap certainly didn't. The competition reaped the benefits of Sunbeam's turmoil and infighting. Head-to-head competitor and South Florida neighbor Windmere-Durable Holdings saw its share price rise to a fifty-two-week high of 37 3/8 in the four months after Sunbeam's multiple merger announcement. By the end of 1998, Sunbeam's stock closed down 83.7 percent for the year while the industry peer group finished up 5.47 percent.[5]

Appendix G

Traditional Wisdom Traps

We have discussed at length the "eat or be eaten" traditional wisdom trap that ambushes many well-intentioned firms, and how this "wisdom" creates a tunnel vision that blocks the panoramic view of the entire array of strategic opportunities available for firms in the consolidating industry. To further challenge the probability of a successful merger or acquisition integration, there are numerous traps into which merging *individuals* can quickly fall. What happens when acquiring managers are convinced the potential loss of revenue, profit, and shareholder value due to merger confusion and turmoil is something that happens to other firms, but *certainly not to theirs?* It is much like an auto accident or fatal disease. Most managers are sure it won't happen to *their* company. Terrible things happen to other firms.

Top organizations, especially market leaders that are widely recognized as good places to work and those that "do the right thing," must take special care to conduct an introspective check before they blindly discount the need for a well-planned and executed merger integration. To assume that merger integration failure and its resulting business impact cannot happen to them is a naïve, potentially arrogant trap. All companies, even top ones, must insure they don't fall into merger failure like so many before them.

How can you conduct an introspective check to find out if you are setting your merger or acquisition up for failure due to a simple lack of understanding of all the potential traps? From our experiences working with individuals in different merger situations, we've gathered the following quotes to demonstrate conventional thinking of those who do not fully understand the absolute imperative for planned merger integration and their own personal roles in its successful implementation. We include statements from both members of the acquiring and target firms to show the wide variety of traps that can undermine the success of the merger. As you read them, look inward to see if you have made or have even thought any of these statements. If you find truth in any of these remarks, you are falling into a conventional wisdom trap. *To fall into a trap is normal*—80 percent of all merging companies stumble into one or more of these traps, while almost 80 percent of all mergers do not meet their financial objectives. Is there a connection? Absolutely!

ACQUIRING FIRM TRAPS

"Our cultures are very similar. We don't expect culture clash."

This statement reflects the most common of all merger traps. Culture clash is a shocking surprise to most combining companies. In reality, even when two organizations *do* have similar cultures, the normal tendency for the integrating organization is to focus on the two firms' differences, not similarities. Without a properly planned and executed merger integration, *culture clash is a predictable outcome.*

"We're a great company to work for. The people of the target firm will think so, too."

Because target employees lose the critical employer-employee trusting bond when they are acquired, many feel sold out and betrayed. They have *not* chosen their new employer. It is natural for target employees not to understand, appreciate, or even care about the good qualities of the acquiring firm. Because their initial emotions following the merger announcement are irrational, they tend to be blind to the positive merits of the acquiring firm.

"The target business fits with ours. We know this industry. We will be successful managers in the new business, too."

Success in an industry does not create the skill set required to ensure success in an acquisition or merger. Chase Manhattan and Chemical Bank were both very successful banks when they merged in 1996. They were well-managed, major players in their industry, with complementary strengths. Chemical was a loan house that focused on capital market strengths and market share. Chase's strength was tied to close client contact, industry focus, and skill with complicated transactions. Synergy was a planned outcome.

However, the reality of the combination was much different from the expectation. Chase bankers thought Chemical bankers were choosing not to leverage Chase's transaction expertise. Chemical bankers were far more formal and looked down upon Chase as too casual in their business approach. Chase bankers felt they were being discounted. Since Chemical bankers outnumbered those from Chase, many Chase bankers saw the entire situation as unacceptable and jumped ship, running to competitor banks. The opportunity for synergy was destroyed.

"We have been successful with other acquisitions. We know how to make acquisitions work."

When Philip Morris acquired Miller Brewing, they far exceeded planned business expectations. Miller market share exploded, growing from number five to number two in just one year. When Philip Morris acquired 7-Up, they had every expectation for a repeat performance, but they failed miserably—the same equation for success just didn't work. Philip Morris failed to recognize and appreciate the uniqueness of each acquisition.

General Electric is one of a select handful of companies that does know how to make mergers work—but their merger integration competency is based on literally *hundreds* of acquisitions. Their expertise did not come easily. It was developed and refined in a series of multiple acquisitions over many years.

"We bought them. They will understand they need to learn our way of doing business."

This is the "buyer is better" trap. It is also a very dangerous assumption because it assumes the acquiring company has nothing to learn from the target. After Disney bought ABC/Capital Cities, Disney communicated their expectations regarding long-range business plans. ABC executives were surprised to learn they were required to formulate five-, ten-, and even fifteen-year plans. Before Disney, ABC had worked hard to cut costs, streamline operations, and move quickly into new markets, *all through one-year plans.* ABC executives now responded by resisting the "exercise" of the long-range plans. They countered Disney's expectation by proclaiming that "Disney just doesn't understand the business."

ABC executives did finally yield to Disney demands, but not without a fight and the loss of many key executives—and not without losing valuable market share. When the merger was finalized, ABC was the number one major television network. Within a few short months it fell behind NBC and CBS. More than three years later, ABC was still floundering in the number three slot.

"We're too busy running the business. We don't have extra time to spend on a highly structured merger integration."

Planned merger integration is a classic ounce of prevention. The organizational effort, time, and money required to repair a poorly executed integration is truly overwhelming when compared to proper up-front planning.

"Merger integration is a human resources issue. Our HR department will take care of the integration."

Integration is *core* work for all business functions involved in melding their organization, systems, people, or best practices with the merger partner. This statement shows how many managers unwittingly abdicate their responsibility to others.

TARGET FIRM TRAPS

"They're in the driver's seat regarding merger integration issues."

This is classic "learned helplessness" or "learned victimization." Effective merger integration happens only when members of both organizations are fully committed to making the merger a success. Unless the target is a basket case that has been saved from bankruptcy, target employees have much to offer and must be an integral part and equal partners in the successful integration. They must learn, understand, and accept their critical role in a successful merger.

———————

"We will lose our jobs. They bought us just to sell us. Our site will be shut down."

The "acquire, slash, and burn" corporate dismantling of the 1970s and 1980s is still vivid in the minds of most people. Target people think an Al Dunlap approach is standard practice in mergers. In most cases, nothing could be further from the truth.

Many mergers and acquisitions in the 1990s were growth driven. While most mergers do experience some planned headcount reduction, job loss due to acquisitions is at its lowest level in over ten years. "The sky is falling" cries of target individuals stem from both normal acquisition emotions and baggage left over from past decades.

———————

"They are forcing this integration too fast."

Because of the great magnitude of change involved in merger integration, many target employees feel the pace of change is breakneck. It may indeed feel too fast, but after merger integration is completed, target employees almost universally agree that a fast pace was the best choice. Merger integration must be planned, organized, and *quick*.

"It will be business as usual."

It will *never* be business as usual, or at least business as it was in the past. Anytime two firms merge their people, facilities, systems, and operations, a new firm and a new business complexion emerges.

"They are a lot like us. The integration shouldn't be a problem."

Even very similar firms experience compatibility problems. Every organization has a unique personality—just like people. And, like the marriage of individuals, corporations also experience an end to the honeymoon. The corporate honeymoon, however, is over much more speedily.

During courting, no one ever dreams that seemingly trivial issues like the proper use of a toothpaste tube or what color to paint the living room could become a source of emotional debate or personal turmoil. Most corporate marriages wander down this same path of nonsensical conflict.

These merger traditional wisdom traps are absolutely real. As you plan for your integration, do not discount any of these statements. They can destroy your chance for merger success. If you or your firm's people, as either the target or acquirer, embrace any of these statements as truths, take special care to learn the foundations and tools of the fast-track system. You must learn that these traps lead your merger along the road to financial failure.

Michael Armstrong's First Eighteen Months at AT&T

November 1997

- Armstrong replaces Robert Allen as CEO.

December

- Sells Universal Card credit card unit to Citibank for $3.5 billion. AT&T will receive up to $1 billion over ten years for the continued use of the AT&T name.

January 1998

- Acquires Teleport Communications for $11.3 billion.
- Announces 14 percent work force reduction through voluntary retirements.

April

- Announces 18 percent increase in first quarter net income.

May

- Announces ten cent per minute flat-rate pricing for wireless phone service with no roaming or long-distance charges.
- Creates alliances with Lycos Inc., Excite Inc., Infoseek Corp., and Yahoo! Inc.

June

- 15,300 managers accept early retirement.
- Acquires Tele-Communications Inc. for $31.8 billion.
- Sells paging unit to Metrocall Inc. for $205 million.

July

- Creates joint venture with British Telecommunications PLC.
- Announces 20 percent increase in second quarter net income.

October

- Acquires Vanguard Cellular Systems for $900 million.
- Introduces Lucky Dog Telephone Co. brand to compete in the "dial around" market.
- Announces 68 percent increase in third quarter net income.

November

- Starts selling the Concert Communications services of British Telecommunications.

December

- Acquires IBM's global networking systems for $5 billion, creating a long-term agreement to buy services from one another.

January 1999

- Creates joint venture agreements with five cable companies that will add another 5 million customers.
- Announces 58 percent increase in fourth quarter net income.

February

- Creates joint venture with Time Warner Inc. for access to Time

Warner's cable customers. Total cable access is now 50 percent of the U.S. market. (Agreement put on hold in 1999.)

• Wins Wal-Mart Stores Inc. contract for prepaid calling cards, displacing MCI WorldCom.

March

• Creates pact that allows a partial merger with Canada's largest provider of local phone service to business—MetroNet Communications Corp.

Notes

Introduction

1. David Kirkpatrick, "No Big Deal: Why Michael Dell Isn't Afraid of the New Compaq," *Fortune*, March 2, 1998, p. 189.
2. "Corporate Scoreboard," *Business Week*, March 1, 1999, p. 86.
3. Tricia Serju-Harris, "Houston-Based Compaq's Top Officials See Cut in Bonuses, Stock Options," *Knight-Ridder/Tribune Business News*, March 11, 1999.
4. Bloomberg News, "IBM Will Provide Services to Dell Computer," *The New York Times*, September 28, 1999, p. C7.
5. Nikhil Deogun, "Europe Catches Merger Fever as Global Volume Sets Record," *The Wall Street Journal*. January 3, 2000, p. R8
6. http://hoovers.com/features/compday.html. (January 16, 2000.)
7. Anne B. Fisher, "How to Make a Merger Work," *Fortune*, January 24, 1994, p. 66; and reference *The Wall Street Journal*, September 18, 1997, p. A1.
8. Mark Sirower, "What Acquiring Minds Need to Know," *The Wall Street Journal*, February 22, 1999, p. A18.
9. Michael E. Porter, "From Competitive Advantage to Corporate Strategy," *Harvard Business Review*, May-June, 1987, p. 43.
10. James Surowiecki, "One More Time: Mergers Are Bad," *The Baltimore Sun*, December 13, 1998, p. 3C.

Chapter 1

1. Williard I. Zangwill, "Models for Successful Mergers," *The Wall Street Journal*, December 18, 1995, p. A14.
2. Robert L. Simison, "Ford to Acquire Volvo's Auto Operations," *The Wall Street Journal*, January 28, 1999, p. A3.
3. GE 1994 Annual Report.

Chapter 2

1. Lee Gomes, "Filling High-Tech Jobs Is Getting Very Tough," *The Wall Street Journal*, December 1, 1997, p. A1.

Chapter 3

1. Roger Enrico and Jesse Kornbluth, *The Other Guy Blinked: How Pepsi Won the Cola Wars* (New York: Bantam Books, 1986), p. 235.
2. Thomas Moore, "He Put the Kick Back into Coke," *Fortune*, October 26, 1987, p. 50.
3. http://biz.yahoo.com/p/w/wmt.html and http://biz.yahoo.com/p/s/s.html, February 24, 2000.

Chapter 4

1. Rebecca Blumenstein, "AT&T's Earnings Soar, Beating Estimates," *The Wall Street Journal*, October 27, 1998, p. A3.
2. Rebecca Blumenstein, "MCI WorldCom Moves Quickly on Costs," *The Wall Street Journal*, December, 1998, p. A3.
3. John J. Keller, "AT&T's Armstrong Now Has Harder Job," *The Wall Street Journal*, May 11, 1998, p. A10.
4. John J. Keller, "AT&T's New Chief Plans Bold Agenda," *The Wall Street Journal*, December 3, 1997, p. A4.
5. Rebecca Blumenstein, "AT&T Net Climbs 41%, Beats Estimates," *The Wall Street Journal*, July 30, 1999, p. B6.
6. Andrea Gabor, *The Man Who Discovered Quality* (New York: Time Books, 1990) p. 139.
7. "Manufacturing Management: Return of the Stopwatch," *The Economist*, January 23, 1993, p. 69.
8. http://www.ford.com/archive/fordmilestones2.html, March 20, 1998.
9. *The Baltimore Sun*, December 4, 1998, p. 2C.
10. Jeffrey Bodenstab, "An Automaker Tries the Dell Way," *The Wall Street Journal*, August 30, 1999, p. A26.
11. Norihiko Shirouzu, "Honda Bucks Industry Wisdom, Aiming to Be Small and Efficient," *The Wall Street Journal*, July 7, 1999, p. A12.

Chapter 5

1. Debra Sparks, "Partners," *Business Week*, October 25, 1999, p. 106.
2. John R. Harbison and Peter Pekar, Jr., "Strategic Togetherness," *Across The Board*, February 1997, p. 56.
3. "MSO Alliances in Cable Future," *Television Digest*, December 15, 1997, p. 10.

4. Scott McCartney, "American Airline's Pilot Sickout Cut Quarterly Profit by Over $200 Million," *The Wall Street Journal,* March 18, 1999, p. A6.

5. Associated Press, "After Anything, Amazon.com to Offer Anywhere," *The Baltimore Sun,* October 4, 1999, p. 3A.

6. Thomas Malnight and Michael Yoshino, Harvard Business School Case—*The Blackstone Group,* in *Business Strategy and Policy: Cases and Readings,* (Acton, Mass.: Copley Publishing Group, 1994), p. 313.

7. Ibid.

8. *Harvard Business Review,* May-June 1990. Reprinted in *Business Strategy and Policy* (New York: McGraw-Hill, 1998), p. 268.

9. http://www.authurandersen.com/bus_info/INDUSTRY/FRANSVCS/Inter.html, April 27, 1998.

10. Gary Hamel, Yves L. Doz, and C. K. Prahalad, "The Core Competence of the Corporation," *Harvard Business Review,* May-June, 1990, p. 79.

11. J. Wiley & Sons, New York, 1996, p. 6.

12. Denis Waitley, *Empires of the Mind: Lessons to Lead and Succeed in a Knowledge-Based World,* (New York: William Morrow, 1995), p. 8.

Chapter 6

1. http://www.us.coopers.com/news/070997.html, March 3, 1998.

2. Jonathan Welsh, "U.S. Office Products Plans to Spin Off Four Operations," *The Wall Street Journal,* January 15, 1998, p. B6.

3. http://biz.yahoo.com/p/c/cexp.html and http://biz.yahoo.com/p/o/ofisd.html, June 6, 1998.

4. Jerry Knight, "Fewer Offerings, Less Gain Dim the Limelight for IPOs," *The Washington Post,* June 1, 1998, p. F7.

5. See *The Wall Street Journal,* October 2, 1997, p. A1.

6. Joann S. Lubin and Bridget O'Brian, "When Disparate Firms Merge, Cultures Often Collide," *The Wall Street Journal,* February 14, 1997, p. A9A.

7. Elizabeth Jensen and Thomas R. King, "World of Disney Isn't So Wonderful for ABC," *The Wall Street Journal,* July 12, 1996, p. B12.

8. Brian Coleman and Gregory L. White, "In High-Tech War Room, Giant Is Born," *The Wall Street Journal,* November 13, 1998, p. B1.

9. Jensen and King, "World of Disney Isn't So Wonderful for ABC."

10. Ronald Grover and Elizabeth Leslie, "The Humbling of Mike Ovitz," *Business Week,* May 27, 1996, p. 64.

11. Bill Atkinson, "Anxiety Prevails at Alex. Brown," *The Baltimore Sun,* November 15, 1998, p. 1A.

12. Christopher Rhoads, "Deutsche Bank to Give BT 'No Autonomy'," *The Wall Street Journal,* December 1, 1998, p. A3.

13. Garry Evans, "The Ospel Interview," *Euromoney,* April 1997, pp. 36–44.

14. Katherine Bruce, "On My Mind," *Fortune,* January 25, 1999, p. 24.

15. Carol J. Loomis, "Citigroup: Scenes from a Merger," *Fortune,* January 11, 1999, p. 77.

Chapter 7

1. Jared Sandberg, "AT&T Seeks Broad Marketing, Technology Alliance with AOL," *The Wall Street Journal,* June 8, 1998, p. B6.

2. Leslie Cauley, "Ma Cable? AT&T Appears Close to a Deal to Acquire TCI for $30 Billion," *The Wall Street Journal,* June 24, 1998, p. A1.

3. Stephen E. Frank, "Citicorp's Decision to Pay High Price for AT&T Card Unit is a Risky Bet," *The Wall Street Journal,* December 18, 1997, p. A4.

4. John J. Keller, "AT&T Chief Halts Hiring, Shifts Budget," *The Wall Street Journal,* December 19, 1997, p. A3.

5. http://finance.yahoo.com/q?s=t&d=2y, February 1, 1999.

6. Leslie Cauley and Rebecca Blumenstein, "AT&T, Time Warner in Cable-TV Accord," *The Wall Street Journal,* February 2, 1999, p. A3, and Rebecca Blumenstein, "AT&T Puts Cable Agreements on Hold," *The Wall Street Journal,* May 20, 1999, p. B9.

7. Linda Grant, "GE's Smart Bomb Strategy," *Fortune,* July 21, 1997, p. 109.

8. http://finance.yahoo.com/q?s=ge&d=3m, January 13, 2000.

9. John A. Byrne, "How Jack Welch Runs GE," *Fortune,* June 8, 1998, p. 93.

10. Jon E. Hilsenrath, "General Electric's GE Capital Targets 40% Asset and Revenue Growth in Asia," *The Wall Street Journal,* June 3, 1998, p. B12B.

11. http://biz.yahoo.com/bw/990212/hj_ge_amer_1.html, February 14, 1999.

Chapter 8

1. "Shareholder Scorecard", *The Wall Street Journal,* February 25, 1999, p. R12.

2. G. Pascal Zachary, "Let's Play Oligopoly," *The Wall Street Journal,* March 8, 1999, p. B1.

Appendix D

1. Jon G. Auerbach, "Fleet Financial Seeks More Acquisitions to Ensure Its Continued Independence," *The Wall Street Journal,* November 24, 1998, p. A24.

2. Ibid.

3. Kara Swisher, "After a Life at Warp Speed, Netscape Logs Off," *The Wall Street Journal,* November 25, 1998, p. B1.

4. Matt Murray and Raju Narisetti, "Bank Mergers Hidden Engine: Technology," *The Wall Street Journal,* April 23, 1998, p. B1.

5. Matt Murray, "Cost of Investing in New Technology Is a Growing Factor in Bank Mergers," *The Wall Street Journal*, November 20, 1997, p. A4.
6. John MacIntyre, "Figuratively Speaking," *Across The Board*, January 1999, p. 17.
7. Joseph Periera, "Lego's Robot Set for Kids Grabs Crowds of Grown-Ups," *The Wall Street Journal*, December 10, 1998, p. B1.
8. Holman W. Jenkins, "Making Sense of Merger Mania," *The Wall Street Journal*, May 13, 1998, p. A23.
9. Robert Langreth and Stephen D. Moore, "Drug Deals Could Drive Rivals to Merge, but Stock Prices and Egos Are Barriers," *The Wall Street Journal*, December 9, 1998, p. A3.
10. Steve Liesman, Christopher Cooper and Allanna Sullivan, "Sinking Prices Prod Exxon, Mobil to Meet At Negotiating Table," *The Wall Street Journal*, November 27, 1998, p. A1.
11. Craig Torres, "Foreigners Snap Up Mexican Companies; Impact Is Enormous, *The Wall Street Journal*, September 30, 1997, p. A1.
12. "More Hospitals Weigh the Urge to Merge," *The Baltimore Sun*, November 24, 1998, p. 14A.
13. Frederic M. Biddle, "Defense-Industry Consolidation May Not Be Over Yet," *The Wall Street Journal*, July 20, 1998, p. B4.
14. John Griffiths, "Global Automotive Group Consolidation Tops $28 bn," *Financial Times*, May 11, 1998, p. 25.
15. Haig Simonian and Nikki Tait, "Motor Merger Talks Set to Gather Pace," *Financial Times*, May 11, 1998, p. 21.
16. Keith Bradsher, "Capacity Glut Likely to Spur More Auto Mergers," *The New York Times*, November 14, 1998, p. 1.
17. Timothy Aeppel, "Whatever Happened to the Old Westinghouse?" *The Wall Street Journal*, October 30, 1998, p. B1.
18. Bernard Wysocki Jr., "In the New Mergers Conglomerates Are Out, Being No. 1 Is In," *The Wall Street Journal*, December 31, 1997, p. A1.
19. GE 1995 Annual Report

Appendix E

1. Greg Schneider, "Boeing Buys McDonnell Douglas," *The Baltimore Sun*, December 16, 1996, p. A1.
2. Ibid.
3. See Roland Henkoff and Janet Guyon, "Boeing's Big Problems," *Fortune*, January 12, 1998, pp. 96–103, for an in-depth analysis of all the production problems in Boeing's manufacturing system.
4. "Hubris at Airbus, Boeing Rebuilds," *The Economist*, November 28, 1998, p. 64.
5. Tricia Campbell, "How Boeing Blew It," *Sales & Marketing Management*, February 1998, pp. 52–57.

6. Ibid.

7. http://quote.yahoo.com/q?s=BA&d=2y (December 12, 1998)

8. Andy Pasztor, "Boeing's Commercial-Jet Production to Get 'Special Evaluation' from FAA," *The Wall Street Journal,* November 30, 1999, p. A3.

Appendix F

1. Patricia Sellers, "Can Chainsaw Al Really Be a Builder?" *Fortune,* January 12, 1998, p. 118, and Michele Marchetti, "Dog Eat Dog World," *Sales & Marketing Management,* January 1998, p. 46.

2. Jonathan R. Lang, "Dangerous Games: Did 'Chainsaw Al' Dunlap Manufacture Sunbeam's Earnings Last Year?" *Barron's,* June 8, 1998, p. 17.

3. Martha Brannigan, "Sunbeam Concedes 1997 Statements May Be Off," *The Wall Street Journal,* July 1, 1997, p. A4.

4. Albert J. Dunlap, *Mean Business: How I Save Bad Companies and Make Good Companies Great* (New York: Fireside, 1997), p. 82.

5. *The Wall Street Journal,* January 4, 1999, p. R28, R37.

Index

Index

About the Authors

THOMAS B. GRUBB is a management consultant based in Hunt Valley, Maryland. Specializing in merger integration and organization performance, his clients include IBM, H.J. Heinz, Kao, Duron, Roche Laboratories, Rhône-Poulenc Rorer Pharmaceuticals, and the U.S. government. Prior to starting his consulting practice, he was a manufacturing manager with The Procter & Gamble Company.

ROBERT B. LAMB is Clinical Professor of Management and Finance at New York University's Stern School of Business. He is a management consultant to major corporations, investment banks, U.S. federal, state, and foreign governments. Professor Lamb has published numerous books on strategic management and finance, including *Running American Business* and *Competitive Strategic Management*. He was Associate Editor of *Fortune*, and he founded the *Journal of Business Strategy* and was its Editor In Chief for thirteen years.

The authors can be reached at *tgrubb@tomgrubbconsulting.com*